ISBN 0 340 07772 7

First published 1973

University of London Press Ltd
St Paul's House, Warwick Lane, London EC4P 4AH
Represented in West Africa by
C. M. Kershaw M.A., P.O. Box 62, Ibadan, Nigeria

Filmset by Keyspools Ltd, Golborne, Lancs
Printed and bound in England by
C. Tinling and Co. Ltd, London and Prescot

A Short History of
West Africa – Book Two

1800 to the present

T A Osae
Headmaster, Prempeh College, Kumasi, Ghana

A T O Odunsi
Vice-Principal, Government College, Ibadan, Nigeria

University of London Press Ltd

Preface

This book is the second volume in the series *A short history of West Africa* designed primarily to meet the requirements of the History of West Africa paper of the School Certificate and General Certificate of Education examinations of the West African Examinations Council. It deals with selected topics roughly from the beginning of the nineteenth century to the present day. As in the case of Book One the treatment of the West African kingdoms and civilizations has been kept free from overstatements. Successes and failures, strong points and weaknesses have been presented as closely as possible to what the available evidence and resources indicate.

We would urge readers to hold back personal sentiments in particular when reading the story of the growth of European rule. After all, the colonial period is the most momentous in the modern history of West Africa. The present independent states of West Africa are nearly all of them colonial creations. Their boundaries have been considered unsatisfactory as they cut across ethnic groups and peoples of common heritage. But what alternative political developments might have emerged if the partition of West Africa had never taken place will always remain uncertain and a subject for speculation far beyond the student of history.

The arrangement of the topics dealt with in the book has been made with a view to presenting as continuous a picture of developments as possible. The teacher should, however, feel free to decide the order in which he wishes to treat them.

It is hoped that the general reader not concerned with public examinations will find the book a handy introduction to historical developments in West Africa over the last two hundred years or so.

We wish to thank and express our deepest appreciation to our numerous friends, those who encouraged us and those who made available to us valuable suggestions and criticisms.

T.A.O.
A.T.O.O.

Acknowledgments

The publishers wish to thank the following for their kind permission to reproduce the photographs included in this book:-

Royal Geographical Society	p 37
Commander Hugh Maclean	p 73
British Museum	p 95
Richard Asare Kwaa	pp 135, 154
Nigerian High Commission	pp 143, 155, 157
Ministry of Home Affairs and Information (Western State, Nigeria)	p 158
Chana Information Services, Accra	pp 151, 153
High Commission for Sierra Leone	pp 153, 155

Contents

1 West Africa at the beginning of the nineteenth century

At the beginning of the nineteenth century nearly every part of West Africa was under the control of its indigenous rulers. By the close of the century, however, there was hardly any area that had not been claimed by Europeans as their colony or sphere of influence. The presence and the ambitions of Europeans should therefore be seen as a most significant factor in the history of West Africa during the century. There were important developments on the purely African scene. There were, for example, struggles by states to defend or extend their boundaries; there were religious revolutions and jihads; there were efforts by states and peoples to make full use of the economic advantages open at the time. However, all such developments were eventually affected by or subjected to the ambitions and schemes of Europeans. West Africa at the end of the nineteenth century looked very different from what it had been at the beginning of it. For this reason it may be useful to begin our study of the century by attempting a brief survey of the general situation at the beginning of it as far as this is possible, so that at the end of the period we may be able to appreciate the changes that had taken place.

By 1800 Europeans of different nationalities had been trading along the entire coastline of West Africa for some three hundred years. Except in Upper Guinea (that is, roughly the area stretching from Cape Blanco to Sierra Leone), where they had taken advantage of the facilities offered by the Senegal and Gambia Rivers as valuable waterways into the interior, by and large the European traders had restricted their activities to a very narrow fringe of coastline. In Lower Guinea in particular (that is, the rest of the West African coast from Sierra Leone to the Cameroons), they hardly ventured more than a few miles outside their trading posts on the coast itself or at the mouths of rivers and creeks. As a rule they kept as close as possible to their forts and trading posts. The result of all this was that, generally speaking, the European traders were lamentably ignorant of the interior of West Africa. It is both significant and interesting that Europeans had been trading in the rivers and creeks of the Niger delta for three hundred years without realising that these were, in fact, the outlets of the great Niger River into the sea. It is not, however, difficult to explain their ignorance of the interior. In the first place there was hardly any need for them to go far inland. The principal articles of trade that they sought after – gold and slaves – were delivered to them at their posts on the coast by African agents and middlemen. It was very rare for Europeans to travel inland to procure slaves themselves. The Africans were, however, as eager to trade as the Europeans. The powerful inland states and kingdoms such as Dahomey, Oyo and Asante took great pains to cut trade paths to the coast to reach the European trading posts and pre-occupied themselves with keeping these paths open. Keeping trade paths free and open was a favourite clause in Afro-European treaties of the nineteenth century. The riverain inhabitants of the Niger delta ran fleets of long canoes which conveyed trade goods down to the European posts at the coast. They maintained war canoes to serve as convoys for the commercial fleets.

Fear for their safety was another important reason that kept the European traders away from the interior. Such fear was more imagined than real, but it was in their minds all the same. In 1779 an English geographical journal had warned would-be travellers to Africa in these words:

'The barrenness in several places, the brutality and savageness of the natives and the ferocity of the innumerable wild beasts in most of its countries [show] that the rays of the sun are here so [hot] and powerful as to dry and burn up the juices of the vegetable and overheat the blood of the animal creation, so that the first was rendered futile and the latter furious.'

The interior must have appeared to the average European trader and visitor to West Africa as a mystery that mattered little. He may have picked up now and then stories about primitive ways or occasionally, perhaps, glimpses of 'barbaric' splendour of African civilizations in the forest. These, however, hardly aroused any particular sense of curiosity in him. Once in a long while an inquisitive trader or official like the Dutchman Bosman or Dalzel would arrive on the coast, take an intelligent interest in the African peoples and their affairs, and make a record of these. Bosman wrote a surprisingly accurate account of States of the Guinea Coast, while Dalzel made a serious attempt in his history of Dahomey to understand and relate the African political events of his time.

However, generally many of the Europeans who visited West Africa to trade or occupy themselves in other ways were not the kind of persons who would be expected to take a keen and intelligent interest in the affairs of the African peoples beyond what was obviously necessary for the promotion of their business. Many of them led monotonous and wretched lives. The

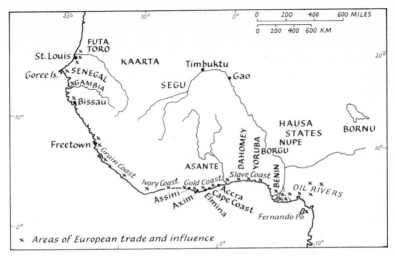

West Africa, c. 1800

employees of trading companies were often paid in trade goods and had to trade on their own account to support themselves. Their living conditions were so hard and pastimes so few that they quite often became so fond of the bottle that they ruined their health. The death rate among Europeans on the coast was shockingly high. The soldiers who were brought to the garrisons in Upper Guinea and the Gold Coast hardly fared any better. Some of them were convicts serving sentences in European prisons from where they had been transported straight to West Africa. One could hardly expect such persons to show any interest in the interior: they did not have the energy for it.

It must be recorded in truth and in fairness, however, that the European trading companies operating on the coast did keep valuable records of happenings among the peoples in the interior when news of these reached them. For example, when wars and succession disputes and conflicts among states in the interior slowed down the flow of trade, these were recorded in the reports sent to the headquarters of the companies in Europe. In this way some valuable historical information has been preserved for our benefit. However, generally this did not go far enough in giving a clear picture of the interior.

Attempts to explore the interior
At the beginning of the nineteenth century the interior of West Africa was still very much considered to be 'dark'. However, this concept was not really because the interior had no bright spots in it; it was largely because those on

the outside had not attempted to enter it to see what it had to show to the world. In the early years of the nineteenth century efforts were made to break through into the interior. Even before the close of the previous century a spirit of inquisitiveness was abroad in Europe concerning the less well-known parts of the world with special reference to Africa. This spirit was of great significance for West Africa during the nineteenth century because it eventually helped to open up the vast area. Typical of this new spirit was the formation in England in 1788 of the African Association by eminent scientists who were particularly interested in biology. The interests of the Association were, in fact, above all botanical, and the search for specimens of exotic plants – especially those of economic value – was vigorously pursued. The African Association in due course became responsible for sending out explorers into the interior of West Africa. The explorers were commissioned to trace the sources, courses and termination of rivers, notably of the Niger. They were also to carry out general surveys and studies of the peoples of the interior. Five years before the close of the eighteenth century a young Scot by name Mungo Park had set out from the Gambia in an attempt to reach the Niger in the Western Sudan and to trace its course if possible. Ten years later, in 1805, the African Association sponsored a second expedition by Mungo Park to the Niger. This expedition which ran into unforseen difficulties ended in the explorer's death at Bussa on the Niger. For the next quarter of a century or so a series of expeditions went out in the quest for the Niger. Expeditions were directed from the West African coast and from North Africa across the Sahara into the Western Sudan. It was not until 1830 that two brothers, John and Richard Lander, sailing from Bussa, made their way slowly and painfully into the Bight of Benin.

At the beginning of the nineteenth century there was a great need to explore the interior of West Africa in order to bring the area into the limelight of world affairs. We cannot help today being astonished at the sheer ignorance on the part of the outside world concerning the interior of Africa. Take for instance the case of the Niger until the Lander brothers brought the long quest for its termination to a successful end. It had been known for centuries that the Niger was the major river in the Western Sudan. In the whole of Africa it was second only to the Nile, the source of which also remained unknown. During the early part of the nineteenth century all sorts of fantastic ideas and theories were entertained concerning the course and termination of the Niger. It was thought by some that it flowed progressively eastward till it mixed with the waters of the Nile. Some said it disappeared somewhere under the hot sands of the Sahara Desert. One acclaimed geographer seriously urged that 'it would be found to end in a great lake in the heart of the continent [of Africa]' where 'it evaporated by the heat of the sun'.

The early years of the nineteenth century witnessed the growing force of a movement which was ultimately to quicken the pace of the process of learning about the interior of Africa. This was the movement to abolish the slave trade and ultimately to emancipate or free slaves. In the 1800s West Africa was still supplying slaves by tens of thousands to the New World annually. However, even by then individual noble-minded persons and small groups of supporters of their ideas and aims had begun a campaign in an attempt to awaken the conscience of Europe and America to the evils of the slave trade. The work of the abolitionists (as those who wanted the slave trade to be abolished or stopped were called) was greatly aided by the fact that economic interests in Britain were gradually changing. Slaves were not vital to the new economic interests. In 1807 the British Parliament, after long debates, passed an Act which declared the slave trade abolished in all British colonies and dependencies throughout the world. This was followed by another equally important Act which aimed at emancipating all existing slaves. Elsewhere in Europe and in America similar measures were adopted. However, the process of giving full expression to the abolition of the slave trade in West Africa proved to be most difficult because it involved vital economic questions. The main business of Europeans and Africans alike in West Africa had been the slave trade. The enslavement of infidels was permissible to Muslims. Some West African states had based their power and economy on the slave trade. All such vested interests would naturally oppose abolition (as indeed they did with vigour), unless other gainful economic avenues were provided as an adequate substitute for the slave trade. This fact was fully appreciated by the British Government and the organizations which had committed themselves to abolition of the slave trade. One realistic approach to the problem was to open ways for legitimate trade as opposed to the slave trade. Hence the redoubled efforts, after the lull in exploration that had immediately followed the tragic end of Mungo Park's second expedition, to open up the interior of West Africa, to learn about it and to establish legitimate trade.

The explorers who did so much to bring conditions in the interior of West Africa to the notice of the outside world were selfless and well-meaning people. Their efforts will deserve praise and commendation for many years to come. However, this should not obscure the plain fact that the promotion of European trade was the ultimate driving force behind most of the expeditions sent into the interior. And this idea was never made secret by those who planned the expeditions of exploration. On his first journey to the Western Sudan in the attempt to solve the problem of the Niger, Mungo Park had referred to 'gold in abundance in all the torrents that flow into the Joliba (i.e. the Niger)'. This made the directors of the African Association very enthusiastic. In 1802 a top official of the Association both urged and warned the British Government concerning the area covering the headwaters of the Rivers Senegal, Gambia and Rio Grande in the following words:

> 'His Majesty's Ministers should . . . hold in mind what will happen, which is that whoever colonises in that part of Africa with spirit will clearly be able to sell colonial produce of all kinds on the European market at a cheaper price from there than any part of the West Indies or America can afford.'

Expansion of European trade was the principal objective behind the expeditions sent out to explore the interior of West Africa in the early decades of the nineteenth century.

The influence of the European presence

It has been pointed out that by the beginning of the nineteenth century Europeans had been present along the West African coast for a little over three hundred years. Quite apart from the main effects of the slave trade with which the reader must be quite familiar by now, the presence of Europeans had involved developments in other respects. Colonization is popularly held to be one of the main results of the presence of Europeans and their interest in West Africa. Quite often this has been thought of as dating right back to the time the Europeans made their first appearance in West Africa. However in fact, except in Upper Guinea, and to be precise in the Senegambia area principally, active colonization by Europeans was not much evident in West Africa. At the beginning of the nineteenth century there was little positive sign as yet of a desire to acquire territories. The European trading companies and interlopers wanted gold, slaves, ivory, pepper, gum and other articles at the greatest possible profit to themselves, but for a long time they appear to have had no wish to saddle themselves with lands or to embroil themselves in the affairs of Africans. The French and the English had at the beginning of the nineteenth century, for commercial and military reasons, developed interests and shown considerable activity in the Senegambia area. The English experiment of the colony of Senegambia in the eighteenth century had proved abortive. Sierra Leone, except for the facilities offered by Freetown as a natural harbour, was considered by the British Government as more or less a liability.

It may be concluded from the observations made so far that the presence of Europeans had been somewhat casual. All the same it can be said that in the areas along the West African coast where there had been considerable contact between Africans and Europeans a number of Africans were beginning to live somewhat differently from the traditional ways characteristic of the majority of their own people. Some Africans on the coast had become quite prosperous by acting as agents and middlemen in the trade with

Europeans. Some such Africans had acquired the habit of dressing like the European traders and had developed a good taste for the strong drinks the white man brought for trade. They could speak the white man's language quite fluently and this could give them a unique status among their own people. This development was noticeable to a considerable extent among the peoples of the Niger delta area. How many such Africans there were in West Africa as a whole by the beginning of the nineteenth century is difficult to say; but the numbers could be appreciable. Perhaps the now popular pidgin English was already gaining ground.

Some European traders had had children by African women and the practice had given rise to a number of hybrids commonly known as mulattos. The mulattos often set the pace in fashion for the small group of African élite. In short it may be noted that by the beginning of the nineteenth century there was developing in areas along the West African coast a growing enlightened class of Africans who were destined to play an important role in the affairs of their localities during the course of the nineteenth century.

The least appreciated of the results of the presence of the Europeans in West Africa is the number of useful plants introduced by them and which had become quite common by the beginning of the nineteenth century. The Portuguese alone are said by Ward to have been responsible for introducing 'oranges, lemons, limes, rice and the sugar-cane from the Far East, and maize, tobacco, pineapple, cassava and guava and other fruits from America'. They are also credited with the introduction of 'cattle to the coastal areas, which were inaccessible to cattle from the northern Sudan because of the tsetse belt.'

Rather unrewarded efforts had been made by this time to win Africans to Christianity which, in their eyes, was the white man's religion. Attempts by the Portuguese to establish the Roman Catholic faith in Benin had met with disappointment. The kings of Warri were Christians during the seventeenth and early eighteenth centuries but only in a nominal fashion. Elsewhere in Lower Guinea the only attempts made by then had been of a very modest nature consisting mainly in the provision of chapels and schools within the forts and castles on the coast for the benefit of members of garrisons and other European residents. It can be claimed that by the beginning of the nineteenth century Christianity had made practically no impact on any peoples in West Africa. In fact the attempts made in the early decades of the century to establish Christianity were generally received with indifference or resisted and sometimes even rejected outright. The one notable exception was Sierra Leone, or more correctly Freetown, where the founding fathers brought over from across the Atlantic had carried with them the Christian faith which accorded well with their European-style living.

A survey of the situation in the interior

It has been observed already that by the beginning of the nineteenth century some areas bordering the coastline of West Africa had had many years of commercial contacts with Europeans. Senegal, the Gambia, the Gold Coast, Whydah, Porto Novo, Lagos, Benin and the Niger delta were among the most favoured centres of trade. All these places were linked to the hinterland by carefully guarded trade paths. There were also long-distance trade routes throughout West Africa. This fact is not much appreciated. As a matter of fact all roads did not lead from the forest to the coast. There were quite significant trade routes linking the states of the forest with the states and peoples of the Western Sudan. The northern factor was a very important element in the economic life of the forest states at this period. For example there was considerable commercial activity between Yorubaland and Hausaland. Benin enjoyed profitable trade with Nupe and northern Yorubaland in beads and cloths, as well as slaves. Dyula traders from the Western Sudan payed regular visits to Asante. Asante traders frequented Kano and other great markets of Hausaland. We can conclude from all this that considerable commercial and economic activities were going on in various parts of West Africa during the early years of the nineteenth century. Later in the century a number of states tried hard to make good the economic losses arising from the abolition of the slave trade. They made efforts to develop alternatives to offset what losses they had suffered. For example, the kings of Dahomey resorted to the cultivation of state farms of oil palm. A similar process was in progress in the Niger delta.

The Western Sudan

The Moroccan invasion of the Western Sudan resulting in the destruction of the power and dominance of Songhai had led to a general decline of economic activity in the area during the seventeenth century. The volume of the trans-Saharan trade had become considerably reduced. The accounts by Es-Sadi, the native Sudanese historian, leave a dismal picture of the Western Sudan in the seventeenth century. However, during the succeeding centuries prosperity had gradually returned to the region. The break-up of the Songhai empire had been followed by the emergence of a number of small states which met the political and economic challenges that faced them. The new states of the Western Sudan such as Kaarta and Segu, as well as the old kingdoms of Mossi and Nupe, were essentially non-Islamic in the sense that Islam was not as influential in the organization of government as it had been in the earlier great states and empires. However, Islam continued to exist as a personal religion for many of the Sudanese peoples.

Certainly at the beginning of the nineteenth century the states in the Western Sudan were by no means weak. The records left by the European explorers who visited the area during this period are revealing and useful. During his second expedition to the Niger in 1805 Mungo Park sailed on the great river for several hundred miles through lands apparently controlled effectively by local kings and chiefs. These rulers insisted on collecting tolls from Mungo Park for using the Niger passing through their territories. This was a well-established system which the explorer could not appreciate. His failure to conform to the customs of the lands in respect of the right of passage contributed to the tragic end of his expedition. It is clear from Mungo Park's accounts that the area through which he sailed on the Niger was the scene of considerable commercial activity. He tells of Moors from North Africa who were hostile to him because they feared that he was a potential threat to their prosperous trans-Saharan trade with the Western Sudan. Writing about the town of Sansanding, Park records that it was 'much resorted to by Moors who bring salt from Beeroo (Walata) and beads and coral from the Mediterranean, to exchange here for gold-dust and cotton'. The African Association estimated the trans-Saharan trade towards the end of the eighteenth century in millions of pounds sterling annually. The Association then dutifully urged that this trade be revolutionized by establishing a trade route from the coast into the interior to divert it to the direct benefit of Europe.

There is clear testimony also of the economic prosperity of Bornu and Hausaland in the accounts recorded by the European explorers who penetrated the region during the early part of the nineteenth century. The explorer Clapperton was highly impressed with the market of Kano in which, Bovil tells us, he found teeming crowds of traders 'from all parts of Africa, from the Mediterranean, and the Mountains of the Moon, and from Sennar and Ashantee'. Clapperton also 'studied the simple looms of the famous weaving industry which supplied markets as far afield as Timbuktu, and the methods of the dyers whose skill was complementary to that of the weavers, and equally valued in foreign markets'. All this was after Usman dan Fodio's jihad which then must have interfered very little with the economic life of the region. Bornu was able to repulse the forces of the Fulani jihad in its early years. Although for many years afterwards the rulers of Bornu and the Sokoto caliphate traded mutual threats, peace prevailed in the area as a whole. In spite of local upheavals, even in spite of dan Fodio's jihad, the Western Sudan enjoyed peace and prosperity in the early decades of the nineteenth century. The states and peoples of the Western Sudan were making significant commercial contacts with North Africa and with the lands to the south.

The states of the forest
The beginning of the nineteenth century was a period of strong governments in the south. A few examples may illustrate this point of view. Although the

second half of the nineteenth century was a period of troubles for the kingdom of Oyo (troubles with which it grappled manfully and successfully) the beginning of the century had definitely seen Oyo at the peak of its power and glory. When the Alafin Abiodun died in about 1810 'he left Oyo an extremely prosperous kingdom with an empire which had been brought under a remarkable degree of centralized administration' (Johnson). The kingdom of Benin is said to have progressively declined from the seventeenth century. However, by the beginning of the nineteenth century Benin, like Oyo, was definitely a powerful and well-ordered kingdom. It still exercized authority over a wide domain and was in control of Lagos to the far west. Dahomey was likewise a great and powerful kingdom. Under a new dynasty from 1818 it had strengthened its army, noted for its fighting qualities, and its corps of redoubtable women warriors. After years of Oyo domination Dahomey at last exploited the difficulties of the Oyo empire and became independent of Oyo. Dahomey had in fact the most centralized and efficient administration in West Africa at this period.

The remaining important forest state, the kingdom of Asante, was also in a strong position. It had established control over a vast area. It had adapted and streamlined its administration to cope with the needs of an ever-growing empire. In the first decade of the century it had fought its rivals, the Fante states, on the coast, and defeated them under the very eyes and professed protection of the British. To the far west in the Senegambia area no great kingdom of the Oyo, Dahomey and Asante type had emerged by the beginning of the nineteenth century. However, here small states of Mandinka, Fulbe, Jola and Mende gave effective governance and met squarely the economic challenges of the time. Some long-distance trading with the Western Sudan dating back to the days of the Mali empire was still in progress.

The main picture that we have before us of West Africa at the beginning of the nineteenth century both in the south and north, and in the east and west, is one of reasonable stability and progress. However, it was to be all different at the end of the century.

Questions

1. Explain why the interior of West Africa remained for a long time unknown to Europeans.
2. What were the main reasons for the attempts to explore the interior of West Africa in the first half of the nineteenth century?
3. What marks had the presence of Europeans left on the peoples of West Africa by the beginning of the nineteenth century?
4. Write briefly on the situation in a) the grassland country and b) the forest areas of West Africa at the beginning of the nineteenth century.

For further reading

Bovill, E. W., *The Niger Explored*, Oxford University Press, 1968.

Johnson, S., *The History of the Yorubas*, Lagos, 1937.

Kirk-Greene, A. H. M., *Barth's Travels in Nigeria*, Oxford University Press, 1962

Sherrard, O. A., *Freedom from Fear, The Slave and his Emancipation* (pp. 120–35), The Bodley Head, London, 1959.

Ward, W. E. F., *A History of Ghana*, Allen and Unwin, 1952.

2 The Fulani jihad and Empire

Events leading to the Jihad

From about the thirteenth century the Fulani began to move progressively eastward from their home in Futa Toro in the region of the Senegal River. This movement took them right across the Western Sudan, some of them reaching as far east as the Cameroons. By the sixteenth century a sizeable Fulani population had become established in various parts of Hausaland, especially in the north-western parts. The Fulani were well-known for their zeal in spreading the Islamic faith and also for their learning. In their ranks were to be found some of the most learned Islamic scholars of the Western Sudan.

There were two main branches of Fulani: the Fulanin Gidda or House Fulani and the Cattle Fulani. The House Fulani were to be found in towns and large population centres throughout Hausaland. Many of them were rich and their reputation for learning, in particular their knowledge of Koranic law, won them influential positions in the courts of the Habe rulers of Hausaland. The Cattle Fulani, on the other hand, were a rather shy and nomadic race devoted to rearing cattle in the countryside. They were not learned or even literate. They were generally not serious Moslems; many of them were actually pagan. Unlike the House Fulani the Cattle Fulani hardly intermarried with the local people among whom they lived and thus maintained the purity of their blood. In spite of these differences there was, however, a general sense of belongingness between the House and the Cattle Fulani. They were bound naturally by common ties of race, language and culture, and besides many Cattle Fulani tended herds which were the property of rich House Fulani. This basis for solidarity was to prove significantly helpful to the Fulani in their jihad or holy war.

During the difficult period following the fall of the Songhai empire, Islam lost much of the political influence it had enjoyed in the Western Sudan. It was not the official religion of the new states that had emerged from the ruins of the Songhai empire. The kings and rulers of the new Sudanese states were often torn between their loyalty to the Islamic religion and to the local pagan practices followed by their subjects. In many cases their royal position derived so much strength from the local pagan customs and practices that even if they personally wanted to do so they did not have the courage to adhere to strict Moslem observances. The only notable exception to this development in the Sudan was Bornu, where Islam continued to be the official state religion and where the kings or Mais were often learned in the Koran.

In the course of the eighteenth century the general lack of zeal for orthodox Islamic observance in the states of the Sudan led to a number of reformist movements. At the very end of the century such a reformist movement took place in Hausaland, finally ending in the Fulani jihad. This momentous development in Northern Nigeria was aided by the career of one of the most remarkable and learned Moslem leaders of the Sudan, Usman dan Fodio.

Usman dan Fodio was a Fulani who traced his descent to immigrants from Futa Toro. He was born at Marata in the northern Hausa State of Gobir. As a young man Fodio travelled to Agades, now situated in the Republic of Niger, where he studied at the feet of a celebrated scholar and teacher called Mallam Jibril. Agades was then one of the leading centres of learning not only of the Sudan but also of the Moslem world. After his studies in Agades, Usman dan Fodio returned to Gobir and settled in Degel as a teacher. He was very much respected and admired by his pupils. He soon became well known at the court of the king of Gobir to whose children he had become a tutor. Fodio's contact with the royal court brought him face to face with the general corruption and impiety characteristic of Habe rule in Hausaland at the time. He was worried about the situation which he often discussed with the many disciples who eventually flocked round him. Things came to a head in 1802 when his former pupil, Yunfa, became king of Gobir on the death of his father Nafata. Yunfa's father, Nafata, had during his reign ordered some drastic reforms in his kingdom which greatly alarmed dan Fodio and his disciples and other followers. Nafata had ordered that his subjects should no longer be converted to Islam. Now Yunfa, when he became king, forbade the men to wear the turban and women to wear the veil. This was seen by dan Fodio and his followers as a calculated attack upon themselves, for the turban and veil, now forbidden, were an important outward identification for them and other true Moslems in Hausaland.

The rift between Yunfa and his former tutor grew wider and wider until Usman dan Fodio was compelled to leave the court for his home town of Degel where he and his followers continued their bitter attacks on Yunfa and Habe misrule. At this stage Yunfa is said to have plotted to kill dan Fodio. The news of this plot became the signal for open revolt which finally touched off the jihad.

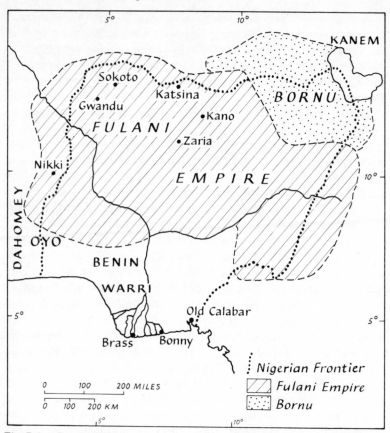

The Fulani Empire and Bornu

General causes of discontent against Habe rule

The discontent which eventually inspired the jihad had the dual purpose of removing Habe misrule and reforming the current Islamic way of life in the Hausa States. Both Moslem and non-Moslem elements, Fulani and Hausa, supported the move to oust the Habe rulers. Habe misrule found expression in heavy and unjust taxation touching various departments of life of the common people. The *gaisuwa*, or giving of presents to superiors, was virtually obligatory. Bribery and corruption in courts of justice was the order of the day. Poor people groaned under heavy market taxes, and the nomadic Fulani particularly resented excessive taxes they were made to pay on their herds. These conditions explain the popularity of Usman dan Fodio when he began to preach against oppressive taxation and economic exploitation that called for immediate redress.

A predominant section of those Hausa who had accepted Islam at all had done so with a mixture of animism and superstition, and their rulers could not help pandering to these indigenous beliefs. To dan Fodio and his disciples this was abominable and the sin deserved to be corrected.

The spread of the jihad

There were three overlapping phases of the jihad. The first phase occurred in the period 1804–1808, during which the Habe kings were defeated and their forces routed. The second phase was a Fulani attack on Bornu (1805–11), and the third and final phase saw the jihadists carrying the banner southwards (1808–1830) in a manner which smacked more of political expansion than of religious fervour.

The first important engagement in the jihad took place in June 1804 when the Fulani, assisted by the Zamfarawa (the people of Zamfara) defeated the forces of Gobir at a place called Tabbin Kwatto. Usman dan Fodio's forces were greatly inspired by this victory, especially as they were by far outnumbered by their foes. The psychological effect of this sweet victory for the Fulani was very significant. Usman dan Fodio, now known to his followers as the Shehu (leader), established a permanent base at Sabongari in Zamfara in 1805. Here he received delegations of the Fulani from various parts of Hausaland and, after blessing flags, handed them to the leaders of the delegations charging them to go forth and carry the holy war to all unbelievers. The response was most enthusiastic. By the end of 1807 the Fulani had conquered and brought a considerable portion of Hausaland under their control. They had subdued the key Hausa States of Zaria, Kano and Katsina. In 1808 they overran Gobir after the king, Yunfa, had been slain in battle. Thus by 1808 a Fulani empire was already firmly established in Hausaland.

The saintly Usman dan Fodio, who was no soldier, had taken practically no part in the fighting himself. His contribution was to inspire the jihad and formulate its philosophy. The directors of the fighting and the chief executives of the jihad and its gains were the Shehu's brother Abdullahi and his son Bello.

The empire so far achieved was divided into two sectors: the Western Sector with Gwandu as its headquarters was placed under Abdullahi, and the Eastern Sector with its headquarters at Sokoto under Bello. The Shehu influenced the administration of the empire by issuing pamphlets and directives exhorting honesty and justice on the part of all in charge of the provinces.

What really happened in this first phase of the Fulani movement was a series of local jihads in Kano, Katsina, Zaria and other Hausa states in which established Fulani lineages emerged as leaders and seized power for themselves as 'Emirs'. The new Fulani 'Emirs' sought to consolidate their own authority in their localities at the expense of the central administration set up at Sokoto. The control from Sokoto over the emirates was generally a loose one. As the jihad spread it lost its original religious fervour. Many of the hordes of people who joined the Shehu's forces were motivated largely by a spirit of adventure and for the sake of plunder. It may be pointed out that not all the Fulani took sides with the Shehu. Many of them remained aloof or actually loyal to the Habe rulers. In the same manner many Hausa remained uncommitted, going about their ordinary daily business during the struggle; some took service under the Shehu.

In 1805 the Fulani attacked Moslem Bornu, partly because the Mai had earlier sent help to Kano and Katsina and partly to reform Islam in Bornu. Led by Ardo Lerlima, some Fulani inside Bornu, taking notice of events in the west, rebelled and in a sharp encounter defeated Mai Ahmad at Nguru. Another Bornu Fulani called Gwani Mukhtar, who had identified himself with the jihad at the very beginning, attacked the pagan areas around Bornu and swept all before him until he reached the Bornu capital of Ngazargamu, which he captured in 1808. Mai Ahmad fled from his capital and implored the help of El Kanemi of Kanem and his famous Kanembu warriors. El Kanemi and his warriors eventually expelled Mukhtar from the capital and later killed him. El Kanemi thus saved Bornu from the jihad. The Fulani, however, were able to maintain a hold over the outer districts of the state. The Shehu recognized Mukhtar's son, Mamman Manga, as leader of the Bornu Fulani and gave him a flag. Manga founded the town of Damaturu and inherited the small emirate of Misau.

Unable to conquer Bornu themselves, the Fulani descended upon the areas to the south and south-west. In the area of Gombe, immediately south of Bornu, an enterprising student of the Shehu called Buba Yero, had begun using force to convert pagans to Islam even before the jihad had started in 1804. He had begun to conquer the pagan tribes of Muri and the neighbouring lands to the east. At the outbreak of the jihad he was given a flag by the Shehu and posted to Gombe. Gombe and the adjoining lands were gradually subdued by Buba Yero.

Another disciple of the Shehu by name Yakubu, after receiving a flag from his old master, carried the jihad into Bauchi. Yakubu is said to be the only non-Fulani of the fourteen flag-bearers commissioned by Usman dan Fodio. He overran all the country around Bauchi and even down to the Benue and Gongola Rivers. Before long the jihadists were in control of Yola, farther south, and its neighbouring lands.

In 1810 a wandering Islamic preacher in Nupe called Mallam Dendo, after attracting a large number of followers to himself, mainly from among the

Fulani living in the Nupe country, carried the jihad into that part of Northern Nigeria. The Nupe resisted Mallam Dendo and his followers resolutely but the Mallam was able to exploit a succession dispute in the country, following the death of the ruler of Nupe in 1818, to advantage. Dendo skilfully eliminated the various contenders to the throne and eventually became the virtual ruler of Nupeland. By the time of Dendo's death in 1832 the Fulani had gained a foothold in Nupe and were in a fairly strong position.

By 1830 the Fulani had conquered the whole of Northern Nigeria with the exception of Bornu, parts of Kebbi and Gobir, and the mountainous areas of the middle states. The Fulani empire thus established even extended beyond the boundaries of the present Northern Nigeria. In the west it covered parts of the north-eastern region of the Republic of Dahomey and the south-eastern corner of the Niger Republic. In the east it covered Adamawa, the northern portion of the Cameroon Republic. It was an impressive empire which compared favourably with the earlier empires of the forest belt of West Africa.

Fulani attacks on the Oyo empire succeeded in Ilorin province and event-ually Old Oyo became part of the Fulani empire. Farther south, however, the tide of Fulani expansion was halted by the decisive victory scored over them at Oshogbo by Ibadan forces.

Administration of the empire
Usman dan Fodio, the Shehu, also declared at the beginning of the jihad as Amir-al-mu'-mini (Commander of the Faithful) remained until his death head of the empire. However, as already pointed out, the chief executives were the Shehu's brother Abdullahi and his son Bello. The empire was largely founded simply by the deposition of defeated Habe kings, and its govern-ment was initially based on the existing system which fortunately was well-organized. The Hausa states, therefore, were not ill-affected by the change of rulers brought about by the jihad. In 1812 the Shehu divided the vast empire between his son and his brother. He had himself in 1809 moved to Sifawa, some forty miles south of Sokoto. From his headquarters at Sokoto, Bello ruled over the eastern areas including Bauchi, Daura, Kano, Katagum, Katsina and Zamfara, while Abdullahi at Gwandu ruled over the western areas consisting of Borgu, Dendi, Ilorin, Liptako and Nupe.

Some alterations were made both in the original state boundaries and government machinery, but no significant changes occurred in the form of taxation which now became based on Islamic law. The whole structure of government remained essentially Hausa. The few changes, however, re-flected the Shehu's own pattern established since the early period of the jihad. The government of the Fulani empire in the early years was marked by stability, justice and honesty. This was largely the result of the inspiration created by the Shehu through the issue of numerous directives on how the empire was to be governed. While the Shehu lived he remained the symbol of unity in the empire. He often resolved difficulties of succession in the emirates by direct intervention. For example, when difficulties arose in Daura he partitioned Daura territory into Daura Town, Daura Zongo and Daura Baure under one Fulani and two Habe rulers respectively.

After dan Fodio's death in 1817, the need for solidarity in the empire became more urgent, for a number of the provincial governors tended to become more independent. The Shehu was succeeded by his son Bello after Abdullahi had made an unsuccessful attempt at the Sultanate. Recognized as the lawful successor of his father, even if less revered, Sultan Bello supervised and regulated the deposition and appointment of emirs. The emirs in person paid half-yearly tributes to Sokoto. Some of the emirates were placed under the special supervision of ministers at Sokoto. Sultan Bello ruled the empire honestly and justly. He avoided the corruption of the Habe regime; he imposed fair taxes and made wise and reasonable laws. So successful was Bello's work that the supremacy of the Sultan of Sokoto as Sarkin Musulmi remained unchallenged until the early twentieth century when the Fulani empire collapsed before British and French colonial ambitions.

When Muhammed Bello died in 1837 he was succeeded by his brother, Abubakr Atiku (1837–42), who was in turn succeeded by Bello's son Aliu Baba (1842–59). The noble ideas of Usman dan Fodio and his son Bello which had inspired good government began to wear thin. The emirs began to raid towns and villages for slaves, creating social difficulties and an unstable political situation. Bribery and corruption became rife again at the courts of many emirs. On the whole, however, the essentials of the administration of the emirates remained intact, were adopted under British rule and have subsisted remarkably to the present day.

Effects of the jihad

The most obvious result of the Fulani jihad was the creation of an impressive empire in Hausaland and the areas immediately around. For the first time this vast area came under a kind of uniform administration with some wholesome results. An efficient administration based on honest rule was attempted and the achievements on the whole were remarkable. For upwards of sixty years remarkable peace prevailed in the empire. This is not to say that all was plain sailing. It is true, however, to say that the area was spared some of the unnecessary and destructive wars of the former times. The various Hausa states that had been at each other's throats in the period of the Habe rulers now lived in peace under the caliphate of Sokoto.

One of the ostensible aims of the jihad was to establish purity in Islamic practices and to convert unbelievers. It is a fact that many converts were won for Islam both by peaceful and forceful means during and probably after the actual period of the jihad. This was a considerable achievement for Islam in Africa. More important perhaps is the fact that a remarkable period of Islamic learning followed the jihad. The scholarly qualities of Usman dan Fodio and of his son and successor, Bello, gave great encouragement to general learning throughout the empire. There was an emergence of intellectual quality unknown before in Hausaland.

We have talked about the adoption of the essentials of Habe administration by the Fulani rulers of the emirates. In this way it may be said that other parts of the empire were made to benefit from a superior system of administration.

There is a good deal to commend the Fulani for; but there is also the other side of the coin. The honesty and fairness of administration as established by the Shehu and his son did not last throughout the whole period of the empire. There were relapses here and there into corruption and the Fulani peace was in later years marred by the violence of strife and slave raids. A more significant development from the Fulani jihad was the destructive disruption it caused in Bornu and the Oyo empire. In the former there was the lamentable spectacle of a Moslem holy war against the leading Moslem state in the Sudan. The jihad contributed to the further decline and eventual collapse of the Bornu empire in spite of the repulse of the jihadists from the kingdom of Bornu proper. In a similar way the activities of the jihadists in the Ilorin province of Oyo, and especially the support given by them to the Kakanfo Afonja, provided the immediate cause of the civil wars in the Oyo empire leading to its final collapse.

For western Africa as a whole it should be noted that the echoes of the Fulani jihad produced serious vibrations. In the various states to the west the example of Usman dan Fodio's jihad led to similar reformist movements and holy wars which gave rise to great religious and political changes. Some of the leaders of the jihads in the west were old disciples of the Shehu or persons who had actually received flags from him to carry out holy wars in the name of Islam.

Questions

1. Why was Usman dan Fodio's jihad popular among the peoples of Hausaland?
2. Why and how did the jihad spread?
3. Give a brief account of events in Bornu in connection with the jihad.
4. Suggest reasons for the success of Fulani rule in the empire.
5. What were the main effects of the jihad?

For further reading

Ajayi, J. F. A. and Espie, J., *A Thousand Years of West African History* (pp. 262–77), Thomas Nelson and Sons,

Crowder, M., *The Story of Nigeria* (pp. 78–95), Faber and Faber, 1962.

3 The Mandinka and Tokolor Empires

The jihad of Seku Ahmadu and the Macina state

Shortly after dan Fodio's jihad, which began in Hausaland in the early years of the nineteenth century, a series of similar Islamic revolutions were started in the west under Muslim reformers and leaders in Macina and the Bambara states. These states were located in the vast country in the shape of a rough bow flanked by the Senegal and Niger Rivers. Macina was inhabited at the beginning of the nineteenth century by a number of different peoples including the Muslim Soninke; the Fulani, some of whom were Muslim and others pagan; and the dominantly pagan Bambara and Bozo. The rulers of Macina belonged to the Fulani clan called Dyalo. The Dyalo were the rivals of another Fulani clan, the Sangare. Seku Ahmadu, a great Muslim leader who was soon to revolutionize both the religious and political life of Macina, belonged to the Sangare Fulani.

Seku Ahmadu was born in the year 1775. He received traditional Muslim education as a boy and when a young man he began to travel extensively. He was present in Hausaland when Usman dan Fodio's jihad started and must have watched its development keenly and derived inspiration from it. When he returned to his native Macina he settled in a small village near the busy commercial and religious centre of Jenne. He was later expelled by the rulers of Jenne, possibly suspected of subversive activities. He moved to a town called Sono in the district of Sebera where he settled down to teaching and soon drew around him a body of enthusiastic disciples. However, at Sebera also Seku Ahmadu had trouble with the ruler of Macina whose son one of his disciples is said to have killed. Things came to a head when the Ardo (the title by which the ruler of Macina was known) called upon the Bambara ruler of Segu to help him avenge the death of his son. Seku Ahmadu was quick to observe that it was improper for the Ardo of Macina as a Muslim to call upon the pagan ruler of Segu to fight against fellow Muslims. Seku Ahmadu subsequently proclaimed a jihad in Macina after sending for flags from Sokoto. The Muslim population of Jenne called upon

Seku Ahmadu to protect them and Ahmadu decided to send representatives to the city to rule it on his behalf. The rulers of Jenne known as the Armar (the name by which the descendants of the Moroccans who had invaded the Western Sudan in the sixteenth and seventeenth centuries were known) naturally opposed Ahmadu's representatives. Ahmadu's forces besieged and finally captured Jenne in 1817. In 1819, following a series of successes in his jihad, Seku Ahmadu set up his capital at Hamdallahi. He made further conquests of the area and soon became the master of an empire which embraced the whole region lying between Jenne and Timbuktu. Seku Ahmadu died in 1844.

Seku Ahmadu's empire was well organized. Its administration was Islamic; perhaps too much so, considering the fact that the territories had a large body of non-Muslim peoples. Legislative and judicial powers were centred in a Grand Council of forty men picked for their learning, assisted by sixty other persons. Final authority rested with a Privy Council of three headed by Seku Ahmadu himself. The empire was divided into provinces each headed by an emir and a qadi (judge). Each province had its own treasury and could raise funds through direct taxes, levy on farm produce, fines and booty derived from fighting.

Seku Ahmadu was succeeded by his son, also called Ahmadu, whom he had nominated as his heir before his death. Ahmadu II ruled till his death in 1852 and was succeeded by his own son who became Ahmadu III. The empire was brought to an end when it was conquered by another great Muslim reformer called Al-Haji Umar.

The jihad of Al-Haji Umar

Al-Haji Umar was born in 1794 in Futa Toro, a region located in the far west in the country where the Senegal River bends south-eastward. He was a Tokolor. He made the pilgrimage in about 1826, when he was in his early thirties. Even before then, he may have been initiated into the Muslim brotherhood known as the Tijani brotherhood or Tijaniyya. The ideas of the Tijaniyya were rival to those of another Muslim brotherhood called Qadiriyya which had taken root in the area during the seventeenth and eighteenth centuries. The Qadiriyya was based on an elite of intellectuals while the Tijaniyya taught that the Muslim faith was basically simple enough to be understood by all who made some effort. Tijaniyya was thus essentially a brotherhood for the privileged and unprivileged alike. It quickly won acceptance in the Western Sudan. Al-Haji Umar, the strong Tijani adherent, found it intolerable to live side by side not only with pagans but also with other Muslims whom he regarded as misdirected and unequal to members of the Tijaniyya.

In about 1842 Al-Haji Umar settled at Jugunko in Futa Jalon which is now in the Republic of Guinea. In the traditional fashion of great Muslim leaders and reformers he surrounded himself with disciples and soon resolved on waging a jihad. He obtained weapons from the coast to arm his disciples and followers who became known as the *tabala*. He had his disciples well schooled in Tijani doctrines. In 1849 he moved from Futa Toro to Dinguiray, a city located near the source of the western arm of the Niger River from its great bend, and just north-west of the city of Kankan. He actually proclaimed a jihad in 1852. He proved unsuccessful in his native Futa Toro where he was repulsed. He suffered a worse setback when he was beaten by the French at a placed called Medina in 1857. Umar's defeat by the French contributed greatly to his failure to secure power in his homeland. He later threw his forces against the Bambara kingdom of Segu which he overran in 1861. He then advanced into the Fulani state of Macina in spite of the fact that it was a Muslim state. Al-Haji Umar justified his action against Macina by claiming that the Macina Muslims were hypocrites because they had sent help to the pagan rulers of Segu who, they claimed, were a 'protectorate' of Macina. Omar argued that, if the Bambara were 'protected' subjects of Macina, they should have been converted before this. In 1862 he entered the city of Hamdallahi to which the defeated king of Segu had fled for shelter. Umar's forces then advanced farther northward, sweeping all before them, until they finally entered and captured Timbuktu. At this point Al-Haji Umar's Tokolor empire covered a vast territory east of the Niger and much of the territory enclosed within the Niger and the Senegal Rivers.

The Muslims of Macina whom Al-Haji Umar had conquered were Qadiri or followers of Qadiriyya. Umar's attempt to impose upon them Tijani doctrines proved his undoing when a combined force of Qadiri in the area rose against him. Al-Haji Umar was killed in the struggle that ensued in 1864. Before he died, Umar had nominated his son Ahmad as his successor and heir to the Tokolor empire. Before long the empire broke up under pressure of French forces closing in on the borders from the west and also due to the rise of a new empire, the Mandinka empire under Samori Toure.

The Mandinka Empire

Mandinka is a linguistic term and the people who speak the language are variously called Malinke, Manding or Mandingo. They form one of the larger groups of the well-known and wide-spread Mande-speaking peoples of the Western Sudan. They inhabit a considerable area roughly in the shape of a horse-shoe starting from the Gambia through south-eastern Senegal regions, bending across the northern and southern sections of the Republics of Guinea and Mali respectively, with a bulge towards northern Sierra Leone, and finally descending into the north-west of the Ivory Coast

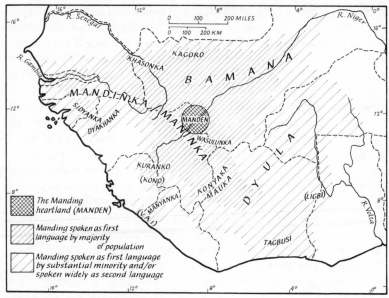

The Manding People and their Language

Republic. The Malinke were the founders and principal peoples of the famous medieval kingdom of Mali. At the beginning of the nineteenth century they still proudly looked back to the glorious days of the Mali empire. After the decline and passing away of the great empires of the Western Sudan, the Malinke, like most other peoples of the area, became broken up into small states, many of which were politically insignificant. Some only served the ordinary everyday needs of a collection of towns and villages. The Malinke remained for many years without any central authority.

One branch of the Malinke called the Dyula had for centuries been famous for their great love of trade, especially long-distance trade which made them familiar figures in many parts of both the grassland and forest regions of West Africa. From their home in the Western Sudan the Dyula travelled far to the west and east and deep down into the forests of the south, buying and selling. They established along the southern fringes of the grassland country Mande-speaking outposts such as Kong, Bondugu, Bona and Begho. At the beginning of the nineteenth century they were still well-known as shrewd traders and skilful craftsmen both in the Western Sudan and outside it. They were to be seen as far afield as in Freetown and on the coast of Liberia, and in Kumasi in the forest of Asante. They were also regular visitors to the land of the Mossi and even farther east to Hausaland. Although the Malinke were broken up into small states and non-political units the widespread commercial activities of the Dyula helped to create an image of the Malinke as a distinct people. It is interesting and perhaps appropriate that when, in the course of the nineteenth century, the small states of Mandinka-speaking peoples were again to be united into a strong Mandinka state and an empire, it should fall to the lot of a Dyula to do so – Samori Toure.

The career of Samori Toure

Samori Toure is a well-known figure in the nineteenth century history of West Africa but rather unfortunately he has been unduly and even notoriously associated with slave-raiding activities. He did raid for slaves but he was essentially and first and foremost a great statesman, soldier and empire-builder. Samori was born about the year 1830. Son of a commoner and an obscure farmer he spent his early years in his native village of Manyambaladugu near the town of Sanankoro. When he was about seventeen years old he gave up the life of a peasant boy to become a real Dyula, that is, a trader. He travelled to the coasts of Sierra Leone and Liberia where he traded in rifles and gunpowder. He took kola from the forests of Liberia and horses from Bobo in Upper Volta. He also traded in slaves. All this gave the young Samori Toure varied and useful experience. The year 1853 was a turning point in his life. One day, while away on long-distance trade, news reached him that the town of Sanankoro had been raided by the troops of Sori Birama, king of Bissandugu, and worse still that his mother had been made captive and taken to Bissandugu. Samori took his courage in his hands and went to Sori Birama offering to serve in his army in return for the freedom of his mother. For seven years Samori served in Sori Birama's army and rose to the position of a commander. He was thus able to add to his already rich experience as a trader that of a professional soldier.

It must have been while serving as a commander in Sori Birama's army that Samori Toure began to think seriously of the plight of disunity among the Malinke peoples. He lamented the fact that there was no single Malinke chief strong enough to impose peace and unity on the whole land of the Malinke. He saw this as a challenge and resolved that he would face it when he had become powerful enough to unite the Malinke. As a first step he surrounded himself with a number of warriors whom he personally led and who gave him unqualified loyalty. Then he declared himself independent of Sori Birama. Samori's iron will and personality won him support from a number of Malinke chiefs who allowed themselves to be persuaded to share Samori's belief in the necessity of Malinke unity. From now on the forces at Samori's disposal grew apace. He made Sanankoro the main base of operations for his ever-growing army.

Samori's aims and activities resemble those of Sundiata who had laid the foundation for the Mali kingdom and empire centuries back. By persuasion, threat and war Samori pushed out from Sanankoro in all directions and brought territory after territory of the Malinke under his control. It has been estimated that by 1879 'the limits of the area under his (Samori's) control extended from Sierra Leone in the west to Ivory Coast in the east, and from a point near Bamako in the north to the Liberian forests in the south' (*Tarikh*). His most significant achievement was the establishment of control over the great trading centre of Kankan in the modern Republic of Guinea. Between 1852 and 1882 Samori Toure succeeded in creating a large empire, the Mandinka empire. This empire included about half of the area of the Western Sudan occupied by the Malinke peoples. It also embraced non-Mandinka areas especially in the country to the north of Ivory Coast and to the north-west of Asante.

Organization of the empire

How did Samori Toure organize this remarkable empire? Some of the methods he adopted were in keeping with traditional patterns of rule during the days of the great empires of the Western Sudan. However, some were his own creation; they were new, revolutionary and remarkably efficient. He used members of his own family as well as trusted friends to command his armies and to rule the territories brought into the Mandinka empire. This was an old mode of organization. Another traditional device was the acquisition of a religious title to enhance and bolster his civil authority. He took the religious title of *almani* which made him not only the civil but also the religious chief of the new Mandinka state. The new methods in his organization of the state and empire were far-reaching. He controlled the local rulers of the amalgamated and conquered lands more rigidly and effectively than had ever been done before in the Western Sudan. Not content with the mere exaction of tax or tribute from the territories under his control, Samori subjected decisions in everyday affairs of these territories either personally to himself or to officials directly appointed by him and responsible to him. He was thus in effective control of all affairs that mattered. The new Mandinka state was divided into provinces which were closely supervised by military governors assisted by qadi or judges. All the important provincial officials were made directly responsible to Samori himself. Each province was divided into districts. The entire organization assumed the form of a pyramid with Samori Toure at the apex holding final authority and overseeing all. In the outlying districts of the empire where use of the military for control was not easy Samori resorted to friendly diplomacy in winning over local rulers.

The chief element in Samori's authority was the army. He was commander-in-chief of the army as well as head of the Mandinka state and empire. His position was secured by the fact that the army remained intensely loyal to him all the time, even in the most trying times of defeat and retreat. Every single soldier wherever he was and under whoever he immediately served owed his allegiance in the first instance to Samori Toure. This was an innovation in the Western Sudan and its advantage was obvious. The soldiers in Samori's armies were carefully trained and were professionals in the true sense. The army was made up largely of captives, mainly young boys, taken from different areas. The soldiers called *sofa* were infantrymen who carried rifles. Quite apart from the trained soldiers of the standing army Samori could press into his service when the need arose reserves from all towns and villages. It is said that one man in ten in every village was liable to service in Samori's army. 'The army marches on its stomach', goes an old saying. Soldiers require large quantities of food and other important supplies to make them fight efficiently all the time. Samori used his past experience as a trader to make careful arrangements for bringing supplies to his soldiers wherever these were required. He maintained a corps of metal workers 'to manufacture cartridge cases and other types of military hardware'. Few African leaders, if any, had made such use of modern methods of organization before Samori Toure's time.

Clash with the French

We cannot tell what the final development of the Mandinka empire under Samori Toure would have been if it had been left alone by outside forces. As it happened it was not left alone. The French began to interfere seriously with Samori's state from 1882. For sixteen years Samori gallantly fought French forces but had to succumb in the end, and the territories of his empire passed under French colonial rule just before the close of the nineteenth century. Once European powers had decided to establish colonies in West Africa in the second half of the nineteenth century it became obvious that they would not tolerate the establishment or existence of strong states such as Samori Toure had succeeded in building. The fate of the Mandinka empire was to be the experience of other West African states. As we shall see in due course, Dahomey, Oyo, Asante and Benin, all of them well-ordered states at the beginning of the nineteenth century, were to fall prey to European colonization during the second half of the century.

Samori Toure's powerful state stood in the way of French colonial designs and ambitions in the Western Sudan. It was France's ultimate ambition to bring under control the whole of the Western Sudan. In 1881 an unfortunate incident provided the French with an occasion and the excuse they probably needed to thrust at Samori's empire. Troops of Samori's army laid siege to Keniera, a small village a few miles away from the town of Siguiri in the Republic of Guinea. The French, who were interested in Siguiri, saw in the siege of Keniera a possible threat to their position. The commander of the

French forces in the area asked Samori to order the withdrawal of his troops from Keniera. Samori's refusal led to incidents in which French and Mandinka forces exchanged shots. Tension mounted in the area and two years later the cutting of a telegraph line which the French had laid between Kita and Bamako, led to more serious clashes between the two forces. The superior weapons of the French forces told badly on Samori's Sofa armies. Samori subsequently avoided pitched battles against the French and resorted largely to surprise raids carried out by small numbers of his troops against French positions. In 1885 the French concentrated large forces at Niagassola with the object of striking decisively at Samori's power or at least of containing his main forces. To avoid total defeat, which he dreaded, Samori began to negotiate with the French for an honourable settlement. The outcome was the treaty of Kenieba-Koura. The treaty proposed that Samori was to rule undisturbed by the French the lands south of the Niger where that river joined another called the Tinkiaso. The lands to the north were to come under French protection. However, Samori stoutly refused to accept a French protectorate of any form over his own territories. The struggle between him and the French thus continued.

Samori Toure under the stress of French attacks now saw the east as the only area left open for further expansion of the Mandinka empire. His attempts to bring under his control the important town of Sikasso led to a long siege by his troops of the town which was well fortified and which its ruler, called Tieba, was determined to defend. When the French began to encourage and give aid to Tieba, Samori was furious and declared the treaty he had signed with the French broken by them. Fresh clashes between Samori's forces and those of the French followed. In 1891 the French mounted their biggest attack yet on the heartland of the Mandinka state. The capital Bissandugu was shortly afterwards taken by French forces who were determined to entrench themselves in that part of Samori's state. Samori and large numbers of the local population began to retreat with the purpose of establishing themselves in a new and safer capital. As they trekked Samori's troops destroyed all before them in the countryside so that nothing of value might be left for the pursuing French forces. This policy, which is known as 'scorched earth', left in its trail wanton destruction and misery. Samori also adopted the practice of making captives of those who were in the way of his retreating armies. This was very unfortunate as it made Samori unpopular among fellow Sudanese and made it possible for his French foes to blacken his image and to justify their own attacks on the lands of the Malinke.

Having been compelled to leave behind the major centres of his empire, Samori Toure established a new capital at Dabakala in 1893 in the northeastern part of the Ivory Coast. In 1894 the French started the final push

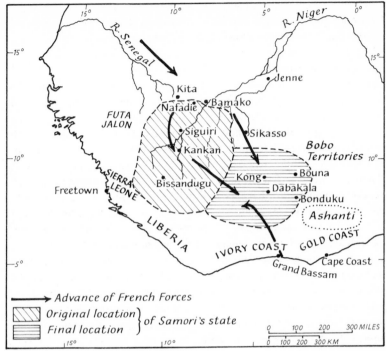

The French campaign against Samori Toure

against Samori. French troops from various French posts in the Western
Sudan and even from Grand Bassam on the coast in the far south began to
converge on Samori's remaining territories. His armies fought back courage-
ously and creditably. Samori slipped out of Dabakala quietly so that the
French forces were for some time unable to make contact with the Malinke
leader. The elusive Samori, however, seeing the writing on the wall, became
frantic. He sought help from the king of the important town of Kong and also
from King Prempeh of far away Asante, but no help could reach Samori. In
sheer desperation he unwisely attacked Kong from which he had lately
sought help. He burnt the city, pillaged the surrounding territory and made
captives of hapless men, women and children to be sold as slaves. His sofa
armies still fought doggedly and Samori repeatedly refused French offers of
protection over his territories. The odds were, however, against the old
campaigner, and the end was in sight. In September 1898 his camp was
surprised by a small French company led by a Captain Gouraud. Samori was
at last taken prisoner. He and some members of his family were first taken to
Kayes and finally exiled to Gabon where Samori died two years later in 1900.
His army was broken up and the men were sent back to their home villages.

The Mandinka empire eventually passed under French rule. French colonialism had triumphed and one of the most determined resistance movements against European colonization in West Africa came to an end.

Samori Toure's failure

Samori Toure's failure in resisting the French is a tragedy. He deserved to succeed, but failed for a number of reasons. Some of the Malinke chiefs failed or refused to support Samori at critical stages in the struggle against the French. This failure or refusal was either the outcome of jealousy on the part of the Malinke chiefs because of the dominant position held by Samori, or the result of the policy of 'divide and rule' vigorously pursued by the French. Sometimes Samori himself made the situation worse by his high-handed measures. We have as an example the case of Tieba, chief of the city of Sikasso. In 1888 Samori laid siege to the city to forestall its capture and control by French forces. Tieba, moved by jealousy and self-interest, had refused to ally himself with Samori in the struggle. The attack on Sikasso cost Samori the lives of 10,000 of his men and all his horses. However, the siege only succeeded in throwing Tieba into the arms of the French with whom he in fact concluded a treaty to the disadvantage of Samori.

During the last years of the struggle the more frustrated Samori became, the less clear judgment he displayed. This situation in the long run worked against his best interests. His attack on Kong illustrates this. The sheer destruction of life and property which characterized this attack alienated those who could have allied themselves with him.

In discussing the main causes of Samori's failure we have to note also that although he fought gallantly he was for the better part of the struggle largely on the defensive. In a sense the French succeeded in their ultimate goal of containing Samori's forces. French forces through military operations and diplomacy were able finally to seal off the north, west and south to Samori. French communication lines on the west from Senegal remained largely intact. The hesitant attitude of the British from Sierra Leone made uncertain Samori's communication and supply lines from the south. In spite of overtures of alliance and support for Samori the British Government in the end failed to honour its word and appears to have been ready to bargain away the Mandinka empire for an understanding with the French elsewhere in West Africa.

In spite of great odds Samori Toure fought well and held on until there was little else to be done. He has been variously judged by both his admirers and critics. His admirers have found in him a great hero who worked and fought hard to build a great empire only to be cheated out of the fruits of his toils both for himself and for the Malinke peoples by cruel French invaders. His critics have tended to dwell too much on the misery in the wake of his campaigns and raids – especially through his 'scorched earth' policy. However the French forces also left a savage record in their treatment of subdued territories and peoples of the Mandinka empire. The one truth is that Samori Toure was a great son and modernizer of Africa. He was compelled by circumstances beyond his control to fight a total war and he made use of some of the disagreeable measures that go with struggles of that nature.

Questions

1. What do you consider important in the career of Seku Ahmadu?
2. What impressions do you have about the administrative arrangements made by Samori Toure for the Mandinka empire?
3. Why was Samori unable to stop the French from overrunning his empire?
4. Do you think it is fair to regard Samori Toure primarily as a slave hunter?

For further reading

Ajayi, J. F. A. and Espie, J., *A Thousand Years of West African History* (pp. 278–83), Thomas Nelson and Sons, 1965.
Tarikh, Vol. 1 No. 4, 1967 'Modernisers in Africa' (pp. 26–42), Longman.
Webster, J. B. and Boahen, A. A., *The Growth of African Civilisation* (pp. 18–45), Longman, 1967.

4 Bornu and the Hausa States

Bornu

Bornu is one of the oldest kingdoms of Western Africa; it boasts of a dynasty that lasted for as long as a thousand years. The Seif dynasty established in the eighth century A.D. survived until the middle of the nineteenth century. The kingdom reached its peak during the reign of its most illustrious king, Idris Alooma (1571–1603). Under Alooma the Bornu empire attained its widest territorial extent. To the north it extended far into the Sahara and to the west it penetrated into Hausaland. Kano and Katsina were under the suzerainty of Bornu.

Idris Alooma was a war lord; he was also a skilful administrator and a modernizer who gave serious attention to the promotion of the prosperity of his kingdom. He worked hard to increase the wealth of his capital and other principal towns of Bornu by encouraging external trade. He cultivated diplomatic ties between Bornu and the North African countries at the other end of the trans-Saharan trade routes. He encouraged learning and ensured the strict observance of Islamic practices. On the whole he was a great son of Africa in his own right and his fame boosted the position of Bornu. Bornu was from Alooma's time and long afterwards the greatest power in the Central Sudan. After the death of Idris Alooma, however, Bornu had to put up with a succession of lesser kings. However, so well had Alooma built up the position of Bornu that for many years after his death the kingdom continued to enjoy a remarkable position of power and influence.

In course of time, however, a progressive decline set in, for great kingdoms can only be sustained by the rule of great kings. The Bornu monarchy in general failed to offer leadership during the eighteenth century. The army was not maintained at its former strength and the outer regions of the empire were left without adequate defence. The Tuareg began to harrass the areas to the north and north-west. Some of the vassal states of the empire reasserted their independence. By the beginning of the nineteenth century Bornu was showing visible signs of a general decline. The one redeeming feature of the old kingdom was that it still remained an important centre of Islamic learning in the Sudan, and Islam was the state religion. The later kings or Mais devoted themselves assiduously to learning as if that was the main preoccupation of the monarchy. This, in brief, was the general situation in Bornu when Usman dan Fodio's jihad began in Hausaland in the opening years of the nineteenth century.

El Kanemi

In 1805 the Fulani in Bornu rallied behind various local leaders and raised a series of rebellions in Bornu in the name of the jihad. The royal forces of Bornu were not prepared for the attacks they were suddenly called upon to deal with. In 1808, one of the leaders of the Fulani rebellion, Gwoni Muktar, actually sacked the Bornu capital of Ngazargamu and forced the Mai to flee to Kanem. The Fulani succeeded in establishing emirates in the western provinces of Bornu. The original kingdom of Bornu itself was only saved by the emergence of a Kanembu leader called El Kanemi. Called upon by the Mai for help, El Kanemi re-organized the royal army and largely with the help of Kanembu warriors was able to drive the Fulani out of the Bornu capital. El Kanemi subsequently became the most influential man in the kingdom of Bornu. He over-shadowed the Mai who now became a figure-head of the Bornu state. El Kanemi built for himself a new seat of government at Kukawa, south-west of Lake Chad.

In 1810 Mai Ahmed of Bornu died and was succeeded by Dunama. Dunama did not make secret his anxiety over the popularity and strength of El Kanemi in Bornu and planned to reduce El Kanemi's position. In an attempt to do this the new Mai played into the hands of those who had little regard for him and he was eventually deposed. He was shortly afterwards restored but in name only. El Kanemi now ruled Bornu as Mai in all but name. He made wise laws and ruled with caution and reason. He introduced reforms in the Islamic religion and his rule proved most beneficial to Bornu. He sought to re-affirm the integrity of the Bornu empire and to this end he re-established Bornu's authority over areas like Kanem and Bagirmi, which were trying to make themselves independent. He firmly united those parts of Bornu which the Fulani had been stopped from over-running.

El Kanemi was not only a brave warrior and a brilliant administrator: he was also a scholar in his own right. There is on record the scholarly corres- pondence he conducted with Sultan Bello of Sokoto on the Fulani jihad against Bornu. The jihad or Moslem holy war was, as a rule, supposed to be waged against unbelievers, not fellow Moslems. This was the main theme of El Kanemi's correspondence with Bello which he elaborated in a masterly manner. Kanemi asked why the Sultan should wage a holy war against

Bornu. The argument between the two Moslem scholars and rulers did not resolve the issue. The correspondence, however, establishes El Kanemi as a scholar of considerable standing and a skilful debater.

Fall of the Seif dynasty

El Kanemi died in 1837 and was succeeded as the virtual ruler of Bornu by his son Omar. There was still a Mai, Ibrahim, but he counted for little or nothing in the effective government of Bornu. In 1846, when a local revolt occurred in the province of Zinder, Mai Ibrahim took advantage of this to raise forces secretly against Omar in order to regain his royal authority. However, Omar took immediate and drastic measures which led to the execution of the Mai. This brought to an inglorious end the Seif dynasty which had ruled Bornu for nearly a thousand years.

Causes of the decline and final collapse

El Kanemi, in spite of his brilliant career, only succeeded in halting for a while the decline of Bornu which had become very noticeable by the beginning of the nineteenth century. What were the underlying factors of this decline?

We have already mentioned the general weakness of the Mais of Bornu during the eighteenth century. These weak Mais were not in the position to check the signs of division which eventually developed in the Bornu society and kingdom. The destructive attacks by the Fulani worsened the situation. One sad outcome of the emergence of El Kanemi as the saviour of Bornu and the virtual ruler of the kingdom and empire was the power struggle which ended in the execution of Mai Ibrahim and the termination of the Seif dynasty.

The decline of Bornu, however, stemmed fundamentally from the gradual decline of the external trade enjoyed by the kingdom. During the heyday of Bornu under Idris Alooma and afterwards, the country enjoyed prosperous trade along the trans-Saharan routes leading into the Central Sudan. A busy trade route linked Bornu to Tripoli in North Africa through Teda country and the Fezzan. Bornu also lay astride another busy pilgrim and trade route between Hausaland and Wadai and Darfur to the east. Trade along both routes brought Bornu considerable prosperity. However, Bornu's external trade was greatly disturbed by the Fulani invasion in the first decade of the nineteenth century. El Kanemi had tried to restore the situation, but after his death diminution of trade started again, this time almost beyond recall.

The activities of Mai Ibrahim ending in his execution were followed by a brief conquest of Bornu and the loss of Bornu territories. The secret force which Mai Ibrahim had wanted to summon to his side against Omar in 1846 really centred round the Kolak or ruler of the country of Wadai. After Ibrahim had been executed by Omar, the Kolak invaded Bornu with an army from Wadai. He sacked and burned the new Bornu capital of Kukawa built by El Kanemi and forced Omar to flee into exile. The Kolak later withdrew his forces from Bornu and agreed to allow Omar to return to his capital but on condition that Bornu accepted the supremacy of Wadai over Kanem and Bagirmi. The Kolak's invasion thus humiliated Bornu and reduced its power in the Central Sudan.

The rest of the story of Bornu's plight in the second half of the nineteenth century can be briefly told. It is a story of growing poverty and foreign domination. In 1851 Barth, a German scholar and traveller in the service of the British Government, on a visit to Bornu wrote significantly about a once rich district of the country: '(This) finest land of Bornu in the proper sense of the word, which once resounded with the voices and bustle of hundreds of towns and villages, has become an impenetrable jungle, the domain of the elephant and the lion, and with no human inhabitants except a few scattered herdsmen or cattle breeders'.

At the very close of the nineteenth century Bornu suffered at the hands of an external invader. During the last years of the century Egypt was faced with a revolt in its colony of the Sudan in the Nile valley, now the Republic of the Sudan. Egyptian armies were engaged in a bitter war against the rebels of the Sudan known as the Madhists on account of the fact that they were led by a saintly Moslem teacher who had taken the title Mahdi. An adventurous Sudanese soldier serving in the war against the Mahdists, a rascal of a kind and a slave dealer called Rabeh, marched westward from the Nile valley with a large army until he reached the Central Sudan. Rabeh and his army quickly conquered Wadai, Bagirmi and Bornu in 1893. He established himself as the virtual ruler of Bornu and began to collect tribute from the provinces of the kingdom. He set up what appears to have been a fairly effective administration. Rabeh was not, however, allowed to enjoy the fruits of his conquest in the Central Sudan. This was the peak period of the partition of Africa by European powers. The British, French and Germans were all laying claims to parts of the Central Sudan. The French in the end took most of the area. Rabeh was killed in an encounter with French forces. The bulk of the old kingdom of Bornu eventually became part of the British Protectorate of Northern Nigeria.

The Hausa States

By 1830 the Fulani conquest of Hausaland was complete except for a few pockets of resistance. For the first time Hausaland as a whole came under a measure of unified government. The former Hausa states now became Fulani emirates who looked to the Sokoto Caliphate for guidance and advice. Each emir was expected twice a year to pay tribute in person to Sokoto or Gwandu.

Any large-scale war, however just its cause and however beneficial its final outcome, is likely to hurt some people. The jihad may have caused hardship to various sections of the Hausa peoples while it lasted, but the fact still remains that on balance Hausaland gained tremendously from Fulani rule. The new administration was generally liberal, honest and efficient, at least during the early years of the empire. Reasonable peace prevailed in Hausaland for many years.

Kano, centre of commerce and industry

The long period of peace promoted two main developments for which Hausaland in general had been noted for hundreds of years – trade and industry. Cities such as Katsina and Kano had from early times been connected with the trans-Saharan trade between North Africa and the Western Sudan. For many years Katsina remained one of the greatest commercial centres not only of Hausaland but of the Western Sudan. It was the terminus of an important and busy trade route leading from Tripoli in North Africa, through Ghadames and Aïr in the Sahara, into Hausaland. However, after the upheaval of the Fulani jihad in the early nineteenth century, Katsina lost its commercial position to Kano which now became the emporium of the Fulani empire.

In 1851 the German scholar and traveller, Henry Barth, whom we have had occasion to mention already, visited Kano, and his accounts of the city-state throw light on the development of trade in Hausaland after the Fulani conquest. Barth estimated the population of the town as about 30,000. It had a great mixture of people including Hausa proper, Kanuri or Bornu people, Fulani, Nupe and Arabs from North Africa. The commercial links of Kano were very extensive indeed. Barth notes in his account that 'the great advantage of Kano is, that commerce and manufactures go hand in hand and that every family has its share in them'. The main products of Kano were high quality cotton cloth, leather sandals, shoes and bags, and tanned hides. Kano cloth was in great demand as far afield as North Africa, Timbuktu and even on the Atlantic coast to the far west. To the south Kano industry supplied Nupe, Ilorin, Dahomey and Togo. The city of Zaria was a great distributing centre for Kano goods going to the south. A variety of European merchandise was received in the markets of Kano. Barth lists among other things 'bleached and unbleached calicoes, and cotton prints from Manchester; French silks and sugar; red cloth from Saxony and other parts of Europe; beads from Venice and Trieste; a very coarse kind of silk from Trieste; common paper with the sign of three moons, looking glasses, needles, and small ware, from Nuremberg; sword blades from Solingen;

Henry Barth

razors from Styria'. Barth also sadly records a visit to a shed in Kano market 'full of half-naked, half-starved slaves torn from their native homes, from their wives or husbands, from their children or parents, arranged in rows like cattle, and staring desparately upon the buyers, anxiously watching into whose hands it should be their destiny to fall'. Apparently these were slaves bought for domestic service.

The end of the Fulani regime

The commercial activities of Kano were made possible largely through the peace that the Fulani bestowed on Hausaland. Zaria and Sokoto and no doubt a number of other towns also enjoyed improved trade. It may be noted, however, that the Hausa states (or more correctly the Fulani emirates) put together constituted a vast area. The commercial and industrial prosperity of Kano, and to a lesser degree of Zaria or Sokoto, was by no means representative of Hausaland. In some states peace and tranquillity did not prevail, at least not for all the inhabitants. In the Emirate of Kontagora, north-east of Bussa, for example, slave-raiding was the order of the day. This was so intensive that the whole area even today remains sparsely populated. It may be noted, however, that most of the slaves were employed on farms in the states to the north. The Emir of Kontagora, when captured by the British towards the end of the century and asked to renounce the slave trade, is reported to have boasted 'I shall die with a slave in my mouth'.

In some of the states to the south there were slave-raiding activities such as those in Kontagora. This was an unfortunate departure from the noble ideals of Usman dan Fodio and Sultan Bello. In spite of all this, however, Fulani rule in Hausaland remained essentially efficient to the very end of the century when the states, one after another, were conquered by the British. The British used as a pretext suppression of slave raids and slavery. Between 1900 and 1903 British-led troops under the general command of Lugard overran the Hausa states. Sokoto, Katsina, Gwandu and Kano were the last to bow before superior British arms. In many cases the emirs of the defeated emirates were compelled to flee from their capitals. In May 1902 the Sultan of Sokoto had sent a defiant letter to Lugard, declaring 'I do not consent that any one from you should ever dwell with us . . . I will have nothing to do with you'. However, in 1903, when it was all over, Lugard had the last word when he dismissed the Fulani empire with these words: 'The Fulani in old times under dan Fodio conquered this country. They took the right to rule over it, to levy taxes, to depose kings and to create kings. They in turn have by defeat lost their rule which has come into the hands of the British'. This was almost exactly a hundred years after the first clash in the jihad of Usman dan Fodio.

Questions

1. Describe the state of affairs in Bornu before the Fulani jihad.
2. What were the main achievements of El Kanemi?
3. How did the Seif dynasty come to an end?
4. Give reasons for the decline of Bornu.
5. Attempt a description of the general situation in the Hausa states about 1850.
6. Describe the importance of the city of Kano after the Fulani jihad.
7. How did the Fulani regime come to an end in Hausaland?

For further reading

Crowder, M., *The Story of Nigeria* (pp. 88–90), Faber and Faber, 1962.
Kirk-Greene, A. H. M., *Barth's Travels in Nigeria* (pp. 137–71), Oxford University Press (Ibadan, Accra), 1962.

5 Sierra Leone, Liberia and Senegal in the nineteenth century

Sierra Leone

The early years

The story of the founding of Freetown has already been told in Book One. From 1787, when the first batch of settlers of African origin landed near the site of Freetown, to the close of the eighteenth century, was a difficult pioneering period for the infant colony of Sierra Leone. Although of African descent, the settlers, most of whom had been born in America, found Africa new and strange. Inadequate preparations had been made against their arrival which happened to coincide with the rainy season. They all suffered great privations and many died. The Sierra Leone Company, founded in 1791 to trade in the area so that it might use its profits for the upkeep of the settlement, was unable to do good business and so lacked the funds necessary to fulfil the responsibility assigned to it. The British Government also was unwilling to make funds available to help the settlers. As if all these troubles were not enough the settlers spent their energies complaining about the constitution under which they were governed and quarrelling with the governor appointed by the Sierra Leone Company to administer the colony. The general state of confusion was heightened in 1794 when the French, who were at war with the British, made a destructive raid on Freetown. Not long after this there followed a revolt by the dissatisfied settlers newly arrived from Nova Scotia. They complained about the whole administration of the colony and were particularly resentful of the decision by the Sierra Leone Company to charge all settlers a quit-rent of one shilling per acre per year in respect of the land allotted to them to cultivate. That the colony was able to survive at all was largely due to the untiring efforts of Zachary Macaulay, governor from 1794 to 1799. The final decision by the British Government to bring the rule of the Sierra Leone Company to an end and establish the settlement as a British Crown Colony in 1808 was timely.

A growing mixed population

At the beginning of the nineteenth century there were three types of settlers in the Colony of Sierra Leone. First, there were the original settlers who had been brought from England in 1787 and their descendants. Secondly, there were the Nova Scotians, Negroes who had fought on the side of the British during the American War of Independence. After the war was over, for fear that these Negroes might be victimized by the government of the newly proclaimed United States of America, the British Government had removed them to Nova Scotia. The promise to give them lands to cultivate was not fulfilled. They found the bitter cold in Nova Scotia almost unbearable. They naturally became discontented and frustrated, and in the end it was arranged that they should be settled in Sierra Leone. The Nova Scotians were hard-working Protestants and their coming to Sierra Leone made a useful addition to the population of the Colony. However, they were independent-minded people – perhaps too much so – who were very jealous of their freedom and of what they considered to be their rights. The third element in the population of Sierra Leone were the Maroons. These were originally runaway slaves in Jamaica who had revolted against the government of the island and for many years had succeeded in maintaining a virtually inde-pendent state of their own in the mountains. They were, however, over-powered by strong government forces in 1795. They were sent to Nova Scotia and finally transported to Sierra Leone escorted by British marines. The Maroons were good fighters and they arrived in Sierra Leone just in time to help to put down the revolt by the Nova Scotians. The earliest arrivals, the Nova Scotians, and the Maroons became known simply as the 'settlers'. It may be pointed out, however, that the original settlers of 1787 were in due course so dispersed that they hardly constituted a clearly distinguishable element in the later population. The 'settlers' par excellence were the Nova Scotians and their descendants.

Although some of the settlers had tried their hands at farming on their arrival in Sierra Leone most of them chose to become traders and clerks in government service during the early years of the nineteenth century. Some became masons and carpenters. A few Africans from the neighbouring countries found their way into Freetown. There were, for example, Africans from the Kru Coast about three hundred miles to the south (later to be known as Liberia). These were employed mainly as sailors and harbour labourers.

After the British Government had passed the act abolishing the slave trade, vigorous attempts were made to discourage the continuation of the slave trade along the entire coast of West Africa. A British squadron patrolled the Gulf of Guinea with orders to capture any slave ships they encountered, free their cargo of slaves, and bring the captains and their crew to be tried and punished. Many slaves freed in this way were brought to Freetown and given a chance to start a new life. These new elements in the population were called 'recaptives' because 'they had first been captured and made slaves, then captured again and made free' (Fyfe). They were distinct from the settlers. The settlers, although of African descent, were American or European in outlook and habits. They wore European clothes; they built houses of wood and stone after the fashions in America and Europe. They were Christians, and many had received some formal education or at least could read and write. The recaptives, on the other hand, were of a purely African background. They were heathen and illiterate. The houses they built in Freetown or in villages near the town were of mud. In the eyes of the recaptives the settlers were more like Europeans than Africans in their ways; they were 'black Europeans'. Every year saw the arrival of more recaptives in Freetown. By 1815 some six thousands of them had already been landed. Some of the recaptives were enlisted into the British army. Recaptive children were apprenticed to settlers and Europeans.

After the long wars between France and Britain were over at last in 1815 with the final defeat of the French emperor, Napoleon Bonaparte, Britain was faced with the problem of what to do with Africans who had rendered various services to the British armies. As in the case of the Nova Scotians it was decided in the end to send these men to the Colony of Sierra Leone. The population of the Colony thus continued to become more and more mixed.

During the 1820s and 1830s thousands of fresh recaptives were brought to Sierra Leone. Many of them were Yoruba and Ibo from Nigeria. It is said that there were as many as seventeen main distinct ethnic groups of recaptives in Sierra Leone. The recaptives tended to live in villages around Freetown according to their linguistic groups. Often these groups elected their own heads or kings. They organized themselves into benevolent societies which afforded their members mutual social services in times of special need such as in sickness, death and loss of employment. The recaptives from Yoruba-land in Western Nigeria, known as Aku, formed the dominant group. The various groups tried to keep peace among their members but unfortunately there was often mutual lack of trust and good faith between one group and the other. This situation led to breaches of the peace. In 1843, for example, a serious riot broke out between the Aku and the Ibo communities.

The recaptives generally occupied a lowly position in Sierra Leonean society during the early years. They were looked down upon by the old settler groups. In the early years also avenues of employment for the recaptives were limited. They took to farming the land around their villages but obtained poor prices for their produce. Many of them subsequently flocked to Freetown itself in search of jobs which did not exist. In the 1830s, however, new economic opportunities suddenly became open to the recaptives. The decision at this time by the British Government to order the seizure of slave ships, even if no slaves were actually found on them but were found carrying equipment for keeping slaves, led to many such ships being brought to Freetown. Their cargoes such as bales of cotton, tobacco and spirits intended to be exchanged for slaves were confiscated and auctioned in Freetown. Recaptives quickly bought up such goods and were able to undersell settler and European traders because they, the recaptives, were able to live simply and cheaply and so reduced their overhead expenses. In this way many recaptives entering the retail business made more and more money. They were then able to buy lands and acquire other forms of permanent property. They gradually raised their standard of living and attained a respectable status in society. The great efforts by Governor Sir Charles MacCarthy (1814–23) to improve the lives of the recaptives through educational facilities and other social services gave the recaptives greater dignity and confidence in themselves as Sierra Leoneans. By the late 1850s the social differences between settlers on one hand and recaptives on the other had become blurred through ever-growing contact between the two groups, especially through intermarriages. In the end settlers and recaptives became merged into the Creole society of Sierra Leone, a society which produced a new civilization in West Africa. For nearly fifty years Creoles led the way in religion, education and in the learned professions and commerce throughout West Africa.

Creole achievement
The thirty years or so after 1860 were years of great Creole achievement. Both at home in Sierra Leone and abroad in other West African territories Creoles showed excellence of service and achievement as doctors, lawyers, teachers, clergymen, traders and public servants. The Creoles loved to live like Europeans, but Creole civilization was essentially original. It was broadly based on Christian living but it was a mixture of European and African culture. It tried to unite the best in European and African cultures. The language of the Creoles was Krio, a convenient mixture of English, Portuguese and to some extent West African languages. This Creole civilization had its foundations in the steady growth of education, adventurism, commercial enterprise and sheer pride in work well done.

Since the governorship of Sir Charles MacCarthy education had become a very important feature in national life in Sierra Leone for all sections of society. An ever-growing number of schools were built each year by churches and missionary bodies for both boys and girls, not only in Freetown but also in other towns and even villages. Secondary schools were opened in 1845. Earlier, in 1827, Fourah Bay had been founded as a teacher training college; in 1876 it achieved the status of a university college and began to prepare candidates for external degrees of the University of Durham in England. For many years Fourah Bay attracted brilliant and ambitious students from all over the West coast of Africa. And from it poured forth streams of qualified personnel for service not only in Sierra Leone itself but also in all parts of West Africa. Fourah Bay sent out teachers, clergymen and civil servants. Besides, many parents and families saved money to send worthy children abroad, especially to Britain, to pursue higher studies. In 1850 John Thorpe returned to Sierra Leone from England after qualifying as the first African lawyer. In 1859 followed J. B. Horton as the first African doctor. Another Creole called Davies qualified as a doctor at the same time as Horton. Soon Sierra Leone was producing enough professionally qualified persons for her own public services as well as for those of other West African territories. In 1861 the Native Pastorate Church, later to be known as the Sierra Leone Church, was established. Creole clergymen, the Rev. James Quaker and the Rev. Oba Moore (of Aku descent) served with distinction as principals of Sierra Leone's leading grammar school. Dr J. F. Easmon, a Creole, was appointed head of the medical service in the Gold Coast after qualifying as a doctor in 1879. He devoted himself to research into malaria and made a valuable contribution to European medical science. Bishop Crowther led an all-Creole staff for missionary work in the states of the Niger Delta. In Ibo and Yoruba countries Creole clergymen worked tirelessly and for many years Creoles formed the majority of missionaries serving in Southern Nigeria.

Another important field for Creole pioneering zeal was commerce. As the Colony of Sierra Leone began to extend progressively into the interior during the second half of the nineteenth century, opportunities became open for Creole merchants and traders. The Creoles became 'a nation of shopkeepers'. They set up business far afield. Creole businessmen operated successfully in Liberia, the Gold Coast, Dahomey, Southern Nigeria and the Cameroons.

The Creoles abroad, fondly called the 'sons abroad', were in constant touch with their families and relatives back home in Sierra Leone. They sent remittances back home, and they returned occasionally to visit relatives and old friends. They sent back their children to be educated at schools in Sierra Leone.

Creole scholars and professional men distinguished themselves and achieved international recognition. We have already mentioned Dr J. F. Easmon who did research into malaria. He was able to isolate blackwater fever as a separate disease, being the first person to recognize this. Creoles led the way in the world of letters in West Africa. A young Creole school teacher A. B. C. Sibthorpe wrote a *History of Sierra Leone* in 1868 and became the first West African to publish a comprehensive history of his country. Another scholar, Edward W. Blyden, produced a history of another kind. Blyden was in fact a Liberian of West Indian birth and upbringing and thus not strictly a Creole, but he lived much of his later life in Freetown. Blyden's objective was 'to emphasize the dignity and accomplishments of the Negro race' and thus opened a question which still engages the attention of African historians and scholars.

For nearly fifty years Creoles led the way in scholarship, trade and the learned professions in West Africa. Their influence was astonishing in relation to their small population. However, Creole achievement fell short in one vital field – agriculture. The few who tried their hand at the development of agriculture did not fare well. They did not obtain good prices for their produce and became discouraged in the end. By the turn of the nineteenth century the golden age of Creoles was almost at an end. Before we examine the main cause for the decline of Creole achievement we may turn to another important development in Sierra Leone – expansion.

Expansion of the Colony

We have so far only been considering the various groups of settlers from whom finally emerged Creole society of Sierra Leone. However, developments in the Colony were greatly influenced by the indigenous peoples of the area. From the early years of the nineteenth century people from the indigenous states of southern Sierra Leone such as the Temne, Lokko and Limba had had ever-increasing contact with the settlers of the Colony. They visited Freetown to buy and sell and sometimes to pick up any jobs that the settlers were prepared to offer them. Boys and girls from these areas were made to serve in the homes of settlers. Settler traders and big merchants set up business in the towns and villages of nearby states. The local states soon began to appreciate the advantages of trade with the Colony, and local chiefs and kings vied with each other to control and conserve for their own peoples as much as possible of this trade. Competition for trade with settlers sometimes led to wars among the states. At first the government of Sierra Leone professed no desire to interfere in the affairs of the local states but in the interest of law and order necessary for the promotion of trade by settlers in the interior it gradually began to adopt measures to bring affairs in the states under some form of control. The Colony Government had no legal nor constitutional rights over the local states, but some form of interference was considered desirable and beneficial for both the Colony and the indigenous peoples.

Missionary bodies followed settler traders (or sometimes actually preceded them) and opened schools for boys and girls in the interior. The Christian gospel was preached to the peoples of the hinterland and churches were established. In this way settler influence penetrated steadily northward, and the practical question of formal expansion of the Colony of Sierra Leone was only a matter of time.

The big merchants of Freetown who were doing flourishing business outside the Crown Colony urged the Sierra Leone Government to extend its authority and control over the areas in the interior where they were trading so that they might have legal protection for their transactions. In the 1840s a prosperous mulatto merchant called Charles Heddle began to organize the production of groundnuts for its valuable oil along the rivers north of the Colony. In 1845 Heddle persuaded Governor William Ferguson – the first governor of Sierra Leone of African descent – to extend the Colony's influence and authority over the main groundnut-producing area for fear that the French might take it. The British Government was, however, very cautious about enlarging the territory of the Colony, and all that it would sanction was the signing of treaties of friendship with the chiefs in the area.

During the second half of the nineteenth century – the heyday of Creole achievement and civilization – more and more traders from the Colony moved farther inland to set up business. They were usually welcomed by the chiefs in the interior because of the general prosperity they brought. However, the Creole traders were regarded as strangers in the interior. And indeed they did look like strangers. Their manners and ways were different: they lived like Europeans and were known among the local peoples as 'white men'. When they had complaints or quarrels with the local chiefs the Creole traders expected protection and support from the Government of the Colony but the governors were generally aware of the limitation of their authority in areas outside the Colony.

A significant development occurred when the outward movement by Creoles reached the land of the Mende in the north-west of Sierra Leone. The Mende were politically well organized. They had large towns surrounded by clusters of villages. They were ruled by a number of chiefs each quite independent of the other; but they had a common bond of being one and the same people. The main town of the Mende was called Taina. The Mende were a warlike people who were often hired by other tribes to fight their wars for them for a fee. It was in such country and among such people that Creole merchants found themselves during the second half of the nineteenth century. Within a few years after 1850 many Creoles, both men and women, had taken up their residence in Mende country for trade. Meanwhile a famous war-chief called Gbanya had extended his power over a large part of Mende country. The Creole traders watched Gbanya with suspicion because of his warlike and over-bearing nature.

In the 1870s and mid-1880s there was a depression, that is a general slackening of trade, in Sierra Leone. This was not a problem that faced

Sierra Leone alone but the Creole traders operating in areas outside the Colony attributed this decline of trade to the many wars fought by the states in the interior. Their complaints about this and their often-repeated demands that the Colony should annex the surrounding territory increased. However, again as in the past the British Government was not interested in annexation because of the trouble and expense such action would entail. Before long, nevertheless, the British Government had to consider seriously the demand for annexation. Beyond Temne and Mende countries there was raging the bitter struggle between Samori Toure and the French. When Samori's forces collapsed before French attacks in the west the British Government became fearful for the fate of Sierra Leone. In the 1880s Freetown had become an important coaling station for British naval merchant ships in West African waters. If Sierra Leone should fall to France, although the danger was never real, it would be bad for the British navy and France might drive the British out of West Africa altogether. If the French did not attack Sierra Leone but hemmed in the Colony by taking all the territories around it, British trade could be killed off in the area. It seemed that the time had at last come for Britain to adopt a new policy towards the Colony of Sierra Leone. The Government of the Colony was accordingly instructed to make treaties with the chiefs in the territories around the Colony. Such treaties were to exclude friendship and understanding between the chiefs and any other European powers.

In 1890 Samori Toure, hard-pressed by French forces, offered some of his conquests to the British to save them from falling under the French protectorate. However, the British Government refused to accept the offer to avoid war with France although British officials and residents in Sierra Leone and the Creoles were eager about the offer. Instead Britain and France agreed to divide the whole country into French and British spheres. The French sphere was to cover the territories 'north of the Scarcies and include the land round the source of the Niger'. The rest was to come under the British. This arrangement, however, did not end disputes between the two powers until 1895 when a final boundary was fixed between the two spheres. This final arrangement gave Sierra Leone its present frontiers.

The Protectorate

In 1896 a British Protectorate was formally proclaimed over all the newly acquired territories. The chiefs in the Protectorate were allowed to continue to rule over their peoples but under the guidance of European District Commissioners. This system of administration followed the well-known 'Indirect Rule'. The Protectorate was divided into five main districts each under a European District Commissioner. The Legislative Council of the Crown Colony of Sierra Leone was empowered to make laws for the Protectorate.

Although the administration of the Protectorate was simple, it still required money to support it. Roads were to be built and a number of essential social services were to be provided. All this, of course, needed money. It was decided that the money needed for the running of the Protectorate should be raised within the Protectorate. In 1898 a tax of five shillings a year was imposed on each house in the Protectorate. This tax which was later referred to as the 'hut tax' was bitterly resented by the people in the Protectorate, goaded on, as the Colony Government believed, by Creoles who had axes to grind. A war, well-known as the Hut Tax War, finally flared up. It took some hard fighting before Government troops could bring the rebellion under control. The Hut Tax War was fought by the Mende, Vai, Loko, Temne, Bulom and Susu peoples. But its hero, the principal 'freedom fighter', was Bai Bureh, war-chief of the Temne. Bai Bureh was accused of murdering Government troops in cold blood and special forces were sent to capture him. He was eventually captured but only after fighting stubbornly. Strange things were said of him; for example, that he could make himself invisible to the enemy and even live under water. The Government decided to keep Bai Bureh well out of the way by deporting him to the Gold Coast.

After the Hut Tax War was over the British Government sent a special Commissioner in the person of Sir David Chalmers to investigate the causes of the war. Charmers reported that the hut tax was the chief cause of the war and recommended that it should be abolished. However, the Governor of the Colony, who had imposed the tax, insisted that the tax was necessary to raise the money needed for development in the Protectorate. In the end the British Government upheld the position taken by the Governor and decided that the hut tax should be retained.

The post-war years were used to improve conditions in the Protectorate. Roads were built. A railway line from Freetown eventually reached the Protectorate. Laws were passed to prevent Creoles from exploiting the people of the Protectorate against bitter opposition by the Creoles. Christian missions extended their activities in the Protectorate and formal education began.

The Creole decline

We now go back to Creole achievement in the nineteenth century. By the close of the century Creole achievement had passed its highest point and the next twenty years or so saw a rather rapid decline in the position of the Creoles. This decline was largely due to factors outside the control of the Creoles.

First and foremost the Government of Sierra Leone adopted a systematic policy aimed at pushing Creoles out of the positions of influence they had held for the better part of the second half of the nineteenth century. This policy was especially pursued by Governor Cardew (appointed in 1894). It has been estimated that in about 1890 there were some forty senior official posts in the Colony. No fewer than half of these were occupied by Creoles. However, in 1912 Creoles held only 15 out of a total of 90 senior posts. What had happened?

Following the far-reaching report of a Select Committee appointed in 1865 to review the state of the British West African territories and dependencies, the British Government had decided to limit its commitments in West Africa with the view to eventually handing over the administration of these territories and dependencies to the Africans themselves. It subsequently embarked upon a policy of encouraging Africans to hold important posts. By the last decade of the nineteenth century, however, the situation had so changed everywhere in West Africa that Europeans were coming to West Africa in greater numbers than ever before. Malaria had been considerably controlled. The partition of West Africa by European powers meant greater activity and greater interest by Europeans. Many Europeans came to West Africa to fill the administrative and other posts that had now become available. This change of policy affected Creoles not only within Sierra Leone but also in the other West African territories where they had been serving for many years. In the Colony of Sierra Leone retiring Creole senior officials were replaced with Europeans to whom also nearly all new posts went. In 1902 Creole pride was badly wounded by the decision that no African government doctor, however qualified, should be senior to a European doctor. This was racial discrimination pure and simple. Then in 1904 followed another decision which segregated European officials from Creoles in Freetown. European officials were to be housed on Hill Station outside Freetown because the site was free from mosquitoes. In the eyes of the Creoles, who had been accustomed in the past to mixing quite freely with Europeans, this amounted to an insult. In any case the result of this step was to reduce the healthy contact between Creoles and Europeans. The British attitude towards the Creoles was dominated by the fact that the British had by the 1880s come to doubt the wisdom of their earlier attempts to encourage Africans to adopt British ways. British prestige was another major factor in the general attempts to weaken Creole influence. The British now saw themselves as a permanent 'ruling race' in West Africa in a way that they had not done in the mid-nineteenth century.

In the Protectorate every attempt was made to exclude Creole influence. Creoles were never appointed District Commissioners or to any senior posts. Creole businessmen were discouraged in various ways from operating in the Protectorate. It was thought that the people of the Protectorate ought to be protected against 'contamination' by Creoles. Later this policy of 'protection' was to be extended to the Northern Territories of the Gold

Coast and Northern Nigeria. However, if anything it only served as a brake on progress and to breed suspicion between southerners and northerners. There was a serious economic aspect of the Creole decline. District Commissioners in the Protectorate are said to have deliberately discouraged Creole businessmen from operating up-country. But there was a more positive disadvantage for Creoles up-country. With the opening up of the interior, big European firms set up business in the Protectorate. They controlled vast capital and were subsequently able to drive to ruin Creole businessmen who could not stand competition. Even in the retail trade Creoles suffered. From about 1890 Syrian and Lebanese traders began to arrive in Freetown in ever-growing numbers. Many of them moved into the Protectorate. Soon the Syrians and Lebanese were able both in the Colony and the Protectorate to drive Creoles out of the retail trade.

The 'sons abroad', that is Creoles working in other West African territories, also fell on evil days. They were removed from senior positions in the public services to make way for European officials. Even in the British territory of Nigeria, Creole agents were expelled from the Royal Niger Company. Senior Creole clergy were removed from missions in the Niger delta.

The result of the progressive Creole decline, especially the way it took place, naturally made the Creoles lose confidence in themselves and become embittered. Financial difficulties made it difficult if not impossible for them to keep up their interest in higher education. In any case there was little point in sacrificing to give higher education to Creole children in the absence of incentives. By 1910 enrolment at Fourah Bay, the great Creole seat of learning, had fallen so low that the closing down of the institution altogether was contemplated.

Liberia

Liberia was founded in the second decade of the nineteenth century in circumstances similar to those that had led to the founding of Sierra Leone in the previous century. During the early years of the nineteenth century the numbers of freed slaves in the United States grew apace. However, the freed slave was generally unable to secure employment that made it possible for him to live decently. Besides, he was not accepted by white American society as a full citizen of the land in spite of what the constitution, the fundamental law of the United States, said about the rights of the individual. However, some white Americans who cared about human problems felt concerned about the plight of the American Negro. In the end an idea was formed that American Negroes could be settled permanently outside the United States, preferably somewhere on the African continent, so that they might live in the conditions of the homeland of their ancestors. The idea was supported by other white Americans who did not care much about the plight of the American Negroes but who felt it offered an opportunity to avoid an embarrassing racial problem in the United States. The seeming success of the British experiment in Sierra Leone gave encouragement to the idea.

In 1816 a number of white Americans came together to form the American Colonization Society to act on the idea of finding new homes for American Negroes in Africa. After preliminary surveys the Society transported nearly ninety free Negroes from the United States to the island of Sherbro on the West African coast south of Sierra Leone. However, the site chosen for a settlement turned out to be unhealthy. It was finally decided to settle subsequent arrivals of Negroes lower down the coast in what is today the Republic of Liberia. A formal settlement was established here in 1822. The new settlement was given the name Liberia, that is to say the land of the free.

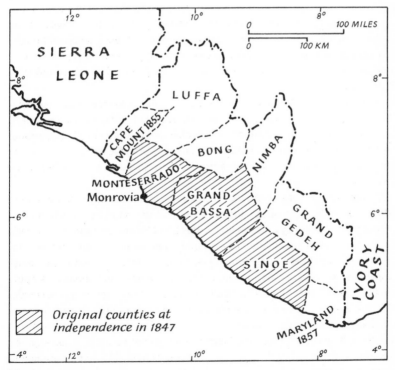

Liberia

Liberia's capital town later came to be called Monrovia after President Monroe of the United States of America.

Progress towards independence

The new state of Liberia was faced with initial troubles similar to those which Sierra Leone had experienced on its establishment. Most of the early settlers came from slavery in America where many, if not most, were born. They were thus more 'westernized' from the start than Freetown Creoles. It became difficult to find gainful employment for all. Those who took to farming did not always make success of it, and the indigenous people of the area began to look at the settlers with suspicion. There were political difficulties too. The period from 1822 to 1837 has been called the colonial period. During these years the American Colonization Society sought to control the government of Liberia, but the settlers wished to manage their own affairs. They demanded to administer their affairs through a free assembly and town councils. The American Colonization Society was not at first disposed to yielding to the settlers' demands. The Society interpreted the persistent demands by the settlers to manage their own affairs as a mark of ingratitude. However, it gave in eventually and in 1837 a new administrative arrangement known as the Commonwealth replaced the purely colonial system. As a result of the new change Liberians virtually gained all power and important positions for themselves in the government except the right to appoint or elect their own governor. This right was still reserved by the Colonization Society.

The Commonwealth embraced the governments of three separate territories that had been created at different times along the coast by the American Colonization Society itself or its subsequent branches: Montserrado, the original settlement founded by the Society; Grand Bassa; and Sinoe. At the head of the Commonwealth administration was a governor assisted by a legislative council.

The establishment of the Commonwealth created among Liberians the desire for a Liberian nation independent and free to act as it wanted and thought fit in all things. However, Liberia's position in international law was not at all clear, at least in the eyes of other nations of the world. Britain, for example, for the sake of her own convenience, refused to recognize Liberia as a state at all. Before the settlements of Liberia were established as a single entity British traders had set up trading posts along the coastline in between the settlements. The British traders chose to ignore customs regulations that the Government of Liberia tried to impose. They even insisted that their consent be sought before the Liberian Government could purchase lands from the Africans living in that section of the coast. The uncompromising attitude of the British traders led to a number of unfortunate and unpleasant incidents. This hostile British attitude further reinforced the desire and demand by Liberians for complete independence. This desire was championed by Joseph Jenkins Roberts, destined to become the first President of the Republic of Liberia.

Roberts was an immigrant from the United States and very light in skin colour; so light, it is said, that but for his woolly hair he could easily pass as a white man. He had distinguished himself in the governments of both the Colonial and Commonwealth periods. Led by Roberts, the Legislative Council of the Commonwealth appealed to the government of the United States to come to the aid of Liberia against the hostile attitude and actions of the British. However, the United States government dragged its feet over the appeal, and in the end Roberts had to persuade his fellow citizens of Liberia to demand independence for Liberia as the only course to ensure the safety of the state of Liberia. In 1845 Roberts finally succeeded in getting the Legislative Council to approach the American Colonization Society for a formal declaration of independence for Liberia. After some hesitation the Society acceded to Liberian independence but insisted upon its rights to all the lands it had purchased with its own funds for the Liberian settlements.

In July 1847 the Legislative Council passed a resolution in favour of independence. A constitutional convention meeting in the same month provided Liberia with a constitution. Independence was formally proclaimed on 26 July 1847. The new government became a Republic and early in 1848 Joseph Jenkins Roberts, who had worked tirelessly to achieve independence, was inaugurated as the first President of the Republic of Liberia. The new Republic included in its coat of arms a dove symbolizing its peaceful disposition and a sailing ship commemorating the arrival of the immigrants from America. The coat of arms carried this inscription beneath it: The love of liberty brought us here.

The new republic had no difficulty in obtaining recognition from the outside world as an independent state. Ironically Britain was the first nation to recognize Liberia as a state in spite of its earlier record of hostility. Britain actually offered Liberia assistance. However, the United States, which had sponsored the founding of Liberia, was unable to accord the new republic recognition, because of the internal racial problems in America, until after Abraham Lincoln and the northern states had won the American Civil War.

The American Colonization Society in due course ceded the territories it had purchased with its own funds to the Republic of Liberia. The Society moreover continued to offer assistance to the newly independent country.

Liberian politics after independence

The political system of the Republic of Liberia was modelled on that of the United States of America. The powers and responsibilities of government were divided among three separate branches: Legislative, Executive and Judicial. The Legislative branch consisted of two Houses, the Senate and the House of Representatives. Two political parties emerged: the True Liberian Party which later became the Republican Party, and the Old Whig Party later the True Whigs.

The Republican Party derived its support mainly from mulattos or light coloured persons of mixed race. Even before independence mulattos had occupied a dominant position in Liberian society. They had become rich or well-to-do through commerce and were the people who mattered in both government and society. They formed a superior caste and stuck together to work for their own interests. The Republicans wished to see their ranks swelled by fresh immigrants of light skin from the United States. Naturally the full-blooded Negroes of darker skin resented and resisted domination by the mulattos. It is unfortunate that Liberia's political parties should have split along lines of the skin colour of its citizens.

At the time of independence all Liberians were, however, unanimous in the election of Joseph Jenkins Roberts as the first President of the Republic. Roberts and the next three presidents came from the Republican Party. The period of Roberts' presidency was generally quiet and peaceful. As we shall see later, this period was one of considerable prosperity for Liberia. Although Roberts was a wise and efficient administrator, he was unable to realize the danger in maintaining mulatto domination of Liberian society and government. He actually encouraged mulatto domination. However, the predominance of mulattos in the Republican Party was in the long run to prove a weakness for the party. The attempts to swell the ranks of the Republicans by encouraging light-skinned immigrants from the United States did not meet with success after the American Civil War (1861–65). And as the death rate among the mulattos was quite high it became clear that before long the Republican Party would decline at least in its numerical strength and give way to its rival party. Since 1877, when the True Whigs gained power, they have not lost it to the present day.

The True Whigs defeated the Republicans in the presidential election of 1869 and their candidate E. J. Roye became President of the Republic. Roye was a full-blooded Negro who had arrived in Liberia in 1846. He had been a successful businessman and held high office first as Speaker of the House of Representatives and then as Chief Justice. Mulattos of the Republican Party who still held posts in the civil service looked down on Roye, first because he was of dark skin and also because he was a new-comer to Liberia.

Roye attempted to open up the interior by plans to build railways and roads. However, the foreign loan that he managed to raise for the project was squandered by corrupt officials and in the end he had little to show for it.

This was unfortunate, for Roye was an enlightened man with vision. When the two years of his office as president came to an end, fearing possible defeat, he extended it to four years contrary to the provisions of the constitution. He thus played into the hands of his enemies. A Republican mob attacked Roye in the presidential mansion and imprisoned him. Roye died shortly after this incident. Joseph Jenkins Roberts, the first president of the Republic, who, after retiring from the presidency, had become principal of Liberia College, returned to office for two more terms as president.

The economic situation

The period 1830–80 saw considerable economic achievement for Liberia or more correctly for the Americo-Liberians (that is, the settlers who had come from the United States, and their descendants). The Americo-Liberians traded in palm oil produced along the Kru Coast. They traded in camwood from which dyes were made. They also cultivated sugar and coffee plantations. Liberian coffee was considered to be among the best in the world. However, the real area for big money for Americo-Liberians lay in overseas trade. Merchant princes like Joseph Jenkins Roberts and E. J. Roye, about whom we have already heard, and many others owned vessels which sailed along the West African coast from one trading post to another. These merchant princes also maintained trading posts in the interior of the country. Many Americo-Liberians who made money through commerce became affluent and lived very well. They built big houses for themselves, especially in Monrovia. They provided facilities for the education of their children. In 1862 Liberia College was founded in Monrovia and it became second only to Fourah Bay College in Freetown in the whole of West Africa. Newspapers were set up and some Liberian scholars produced literary works of an appreciable standard. However, on the whole the scholars and professional men of Liberia hardly exhibited the brilliance characteristic of the Creoles of Sierra Leone.

About 1880 the economic prosperity enjoyed by Liberians and the resulting social and cultural progress began to wane. What were the main causes of this decline?

Firstly, Liberia was caught up in a world-wide depression which occurred in the last two decades of the nineteenth century. Trade in Europe in general slumped and the trading activities of the merchant princes of Liberia were subsequently affected.

Secondly, as we shall discuss fully in a later chapter, the last quarter of the nineteenth century saw the creation of a number of colonies by European powers in West Africa. The colonizing powers adopted inward-looking policies towards their various colonies. Their commercial activities were centred principally on their respective colonies to the exclusion of other areas of West Africa. Liberia was left in the cold by the European nations which had in former times traded with her.

Thirdly, the United States, which could have been expected to come to the aid of Liberia by fostering trade with her, actually abandoned the trade in West Africa to the European colonial powers. She rather concentrated on trade with the Latin American countries to the south. Liberian coffee which had been introduced into Brazil, flourished so well there that it captured the market of the United States. Liberian coffee plantation owners suffered. It looked as if destiny itself was against Liberia. The replacement of beet sugar for cane sugar at the time also worked against sugar production in Liberia. At the same time the Liberian camwood trade fell on bad days as man-made substitutes were developed in place of natural dyes.

From 1900 to 1914 it looked as if German commercial interests in Liberia would save the Republic from complete economic ruin. Germany, unlike Britain and France, had established only two colonies in West Africa and four on the whole African continent. She thus wanted to obtain tropical goods from Liberia to supplement her colonial supplies. A number of German firms began various enterprises in Liberia. The sons of the former merchant princes of Liberia contented themselves with acting as agents for the various German firms. However, this salvage of the Liberian economy was shortlived. The First World War came and the Germans had to back out of West Africa. Liberia quickly drifted back to its position of economic insignificance characteristic of the period 1880 to 1900. All that educated Liberians could now look forward to was employment in the Civil Service, in the church and in teaching. The Civil Service in particular was deliberately overstaffed to create jobs for the sons of leading Liberian families. The ruling True Whig Party indulged in patronage more than ever before, and politics virtually became a profession. Liberia became poor and weak, and the merchant ships calling at other West African ports by-passed the Liberian chief port of Monrovia.

National unity

Unifying the various sections of Liberian society proved to be a difficult and protracted problem. Even among Americo-Liberians there were sharp differences between mulattos and Negroes, as we have already seen. These differences did not help the creation of unified society. While the Republican Party remained in power, the mulattos used all kinds of discriminatory measures to advance their own interests. They were even accused of using the courts in an improper manner to suppress their opponents, the Whigs. When Joseph Jenkins Roberts became principal of Liberia College he is said to have admitted only mulatto students. Then when the Whigs came to power in 1869 it was their turn to discriminate against mulatto students. The True Whigs appointed only members of their party to the staff of the College. A close friend and staunch supporter of President Roye called Blyden, when he became principal of the College, made a point of admitting only Negro students; so now the boot was on the other foot.

It was not only within the ranks of the Americo-Liberians that disharmony showed itself in Liberian society. Between Americo-Liberians and the indigenous Africans (whom the Americo-Liberians referred to as *natives*) all was far from well. The Americo-Liberians considered themselves as a group to be more civilized than the aboriginal Africans whom they looked down upon, and towards whom they adopted a paternalistic attitude.

Who were these other Liberians distinct from the Americo-Liberians? Right from the beginning of the settlements sponsored by the American Society of Colonization Africans from the neighbouring territories had progressively come under the government and control of the settlements. Africans whose lands had been acquired through treaties were brought into closer union with the Liberian Government. However, some of the Africans had real grievances. At the time of the founding of Liberia some African chiefs and their peoples had been forcibly dispossessed of their lands. What really happened over the years was that the Africans were pushed out of the coastal areas either by force or persuasion to make room for the settlers. In 1855 as many as 2,000 Grebos were forced out of their home in the Cape Palmas area at gun point. It should be pointed out that the African peoples with whom the Americo-Liberians were dealing were not simple aborigines, the so-called tribesmen. Among them were such peoples as the Vai, Malinke, Grebo, and the Kru, all very active and proud peoples with past history and performance they very much cherished. The Kru in particular had been in close contact with Europeans ever since the sixteenth century and were well known for their services on many European vessels.

It will be seen that the way to true national progress in Liberia lay in bringing together all the various elements in Liberian society, both Americo-Liberians and Africans. Joseph Jenkins Roberts had a vision of the influence that Americo-Liberians could exert on Liberians as a whole, but he was in no doubt about the magnitude of the problem. He had stated soon after being inaugurated as President of the Republic of Liberia:

'It is extremely desirable that the whole aboriginal population of the Republic should be drawn as rapidly as possible within the circle of civilization and be fitted by suitable educational training for all the duties and social life; and thus we too [the Americo-Liberians] shall be exerting a hallowed influence upon the tribes of our far interior. When we contemplate the magnitude of this work in comparision with the means at our command for its energetic protection it is not surprising that we show at times despondency . . . for the great undertaking.'

These words sound rather paternalistic but on the whole the Africans were prepared to sacrifice even portions of their lands in return for education for their children. They generally appreciated the blessings of trade and contact with the Americo-Liberians. During the fifty years of economic prosperity for Liberia the African peoples remained quiet under the rule and control of the Liberian Government. However, after the period of prosperity was over and things were difficult for the Americo-Liberians themselves, the Africans became disillusioned and restive. Discrimination against them especially in economic matters, heavy taxation imposed by the Liberian Government in its general search for funds, and a general feeling of injustice on the part of the Africans led to a number of African revolts against the Liberian Government. Against this general background, however, steady progress in assimilation of the Africans took place under the True Whigs. Intermarriage involving Americo-Liberians and Africans and growing educational facilities for Africans began to bridge the gap between the two sections of Liberian society and to work towards national unity.

What was Liberia's role in West Africa in general? The citizens of the Republic have always prided themselves on Liberia being by far the oldest independent state in West Africa. It is on record that when the French occupied Abomey, capital of the kingdom of Dahomey, in November 1892, a Liberian newspaper strongly criticized the action and sent a delegation to Paris to protest. This was laudable and, on the whole, Liberia was a symbol and example of independence to other West Africans. However, the Government of the Republic had a very difficult task establishing order in its own house. It had a corrupt Afro-American clique which oppressed the indigenous peoples of the hinterland, which it in fact only very imperfectly controlled.

Senegal

Senegal is in some ways a unique country in West Africa. During the French colonial period it was the most affected by the policy of assimilation, that is, making the colonial peoples as French as possible in their ways of doing things and in their outlook in general. It still bears the marks of that policy. Senegal has always had a comparatively large French population. Just before independence Dakar, the Senegalese capital, alone had a population of nearly 30,000 Frenchmen. Another important fact about the country is that relations between the various ethnic groups are as harmonious as anywhere else in West Africa. Senegal has thus been spared the tribal feuds and conflicts which have plagued some other West African countries. Although the indigenous population is overwhelmingly Moslem, there has always been remarkable co-operation between Moslems and the Christian minority.

The main ethnic groups of Senegal are, in the order of size of population, the Wolof (whose language is a lingua franca), Sere, Fula, Tokolor, Diola and Mandingo. In times past some of these peoples had established effective kingdoms in their areas; however, there was no political development in Senegal comparable to the larger West African kingdoms such as Oyo, Dahomey, Asante and Benin. The power and position of the kingdoms and chiefdoms of Senegal waned under French colonial administration which did not encourage indigenous rulers as the British did.

French connection with Senegal dates back to the seventeenth century. In 1659 a Frenchman called Caullier founded the town of St Louis on a small island at the mouth of the Senegal River. The town quickly grew into a prosperous trading centre and became the most important French post on the West African coast. Farther down the coast the French established another settlement on the island of Goree. Meanwhile they had begun to explore the Senegal River which proved to be a valuable waterway into the interior.

During the period 1756–63 when Britain and France were engaged in the conflict known as the Seven Years' War, St Louis fell into the hands of the British but was eventually returned to France in 1779. The town was to fall again to the British during the Napoleonic wars (1801–14), again to be returned to France after the wars in 1817. Active French colonization of Senegal may be said to have begun from this point in time. First, an attempt was made to settle about 200 Frenchmen on the present site of Dakar which was then a small village. Second, France acquired a number of concessions of land from local chiefs in the immediate hinterland of St Louis for the cultivation of olives, coconuts and coffee. These efforts, however, did not bear fruit. However, the number of Frenchmen in Senegal increased gradually and in course of time there emerged a considerable population of mulattos. These mulattos were accorded the status of French citizens. And so were a number of indigenous Senegalese, especially the products of the few schools that had been established in the main centres where Frenchmen lived. Eventually the entire coastal areas where French influence had been steadily established were organised into four principal municipalities. These were centred round the key towns of St Louis, Goree, Dakar and Rufisque. The area covered by them constituted the French colony of Senegal. The outer areas of Senegal did not form part of the colony although French influence gradually penetrated those areas.

The Senegalese, who were granted French citizenship as well as the mulattos, were given the right of voting like any other French citizen in

France. They were represented in the French National Assembly in Paris by a deputy as early as 1848. It has to be pointed out, however, that this became a permanent feature of the French Constitution only from 1879.

Faidherbe and Senegal

In 1852 Louis Napoleon, who had earlier become President of the Second Republic of France, declared himself Emperor Napoleon III. The period of his reign, 1852–70, has been called the Second Empire.

During the early years of the Second Empire, France began active colonial expansion in Africa south of the Sahara. In 1854 a very energetic Frenchman called Louis Faidherbe was appointed Governor of Senegal. His eleven years of service in Senegal laid the foundation for France's West African empire. He set up a Corps of Senegalese troops who fought numerous campaigns to extend French rule in the Sene-Gambia area and beyond. It was these troops which fought and repulsed the reformist Tokolor leader Al Haji Omar about whom we read in Chapter Three. By conquests and by signing treaties with local chiefs, Faidherbe was able to bring about a third of the present size of Senegal under French rule. He established a firm and efficient administration and brought about remarkable progress. He expanded facilities for education. He even set up Moslem schools for Moslem children whose parents were not happy about sending them to the ordinary schools. He saw to it that promising students were awarded scholarships to enable them to study in secondary schools in France. Technical schools were opened in Dakar for training Senegalese children in elementary technical skills. The period of his administration saw the establishment of a bank in Dakar. He was a remarkable man.

Faidherbe's Senegal consisted of two sections: the Colony and the outer regions which formed a kind of Protectorate. Within the Colony itself Faidherbe encouraged the progress of the policy of assimilation. But even so, at the end of his period in 1865, out of a total population of 150,000 in the Colony, only 15,000 Senegalese had become French citizens; and these were to be found mainly in the original French settlements of St Louis, Goree and Dakar. The inhabitants of the Protectorate, who were known as *subjects* (as opposed to French citizens), were generally subjected to a harsh system of rule. They were not allowed to leave their own areas. They were subjected to the old French practice of forced labour called the *corvée* by which whole villages were driven to partake in public works such as road-building, without pay.

Négritude

The policy of assimilation was not consistently followed by the French in Senegal. Although French and Senegalese showed polite neighbourliness towards each other there was not as a rule very great warmth between the two races on the personal level. During the last part of the nineteenth century there were signs that Frenchmen in Senegal did not want assimilation to go ahead too quickly. As education for the Senegalese increased, growing numbers of Senegalese who had acquired French citizenship became available to fill positions that had been occupied by Frenchmen in the past. Frenchmen were particularly incensed by the relaxation made for the Senegalese in the normal regulations for acquiring French citizenship. For example, contrary to the original provisions, Moslems, men with more than one wife, and illiterate persons were granted French citizenship. The Frenchmen pointed out that Senegalese who had become French citizens such as those mentioned had, as it were, the best of both worlds. They did what ordinary French *subjects* would do as well as enjoying the privileges of French citizens. This was not fair, they said.

From the 1930s there developed a reaction against assimilation ironically by the indigenous Senegalese. This reaction came from Senegalese of high standing who had become most assimilated, the products of universities in France. Leopold Senghor, the present President of the Republic of Senegal, was the leading exponent of the reaction against assimilation.

Leopold Senghor and those who thought like him began to appreciate the qualities and worth of African culture. They rejected the old notion that Africa had no history worthy of study and that the African race had made no contribution to world civilization. This new movement which saw merit and honour in African culture and things African generally was given the name *Négritude*. The movement sought to establish the dignity of the African personality and to call upon educated Africans to rediscover themselves by returning to the essentially African things which assimilation had made them reject: African art, music and history became worthy subjects of study. To arouse support, Négritude tried to show how sadly Africa had been exploited by the white men and pictured a goal of glory and freedom for Africa.

However, in spite of the eloquent appeal for self-assertion by the African, Négritude did not in political terms seek complete independence for Senegal. Although Senghor and his friends and supporters wished to see the Senegalese, or for that matter any other peoples under French colonial rule, become responsible for ordering their own lives and affairs, they did not advocate a break with France.

The ideas of Négritude were relevant and meaningful in Senegal and in the rest of French West Africa where the policy of assimilation was robbing the African of his real personality. In British West Africa the urgency of the appeal of Négritude was lost because, thanks to general British policy, assimilation was never an issue under British rule.

Groundnuts

We should not leave Senegal without saying something about groundnuts, or peanuts as they are sometimes called, for the groundnut has for many years been the basis of the economy of the country. Earlier in the nineteenth century the French had tried to grow oil palm in Senegal but without much success. It was not only because competition from palm oil from the Ivory Coast, Dahomey and Nigeria was too great. Frenchmen did not like the soap of yellow colour such as was produced from palm oil. Then the soap makers of the French city of Marseilles discovered that if olive oil was mixed with groundnut oil a blue marble soap was the result. From then onwards the cultivation of peanuts grew apace in Senegal. And the light sandy soil of Senegal was found most suitable for groundnuts. St Louis and Goree became great centres of groundnut trade. From the two areas the cultivation of groundnuts spread quickly inland and into the Gambia.

The groundnut trade eventually transformed Senegal into a bustling colony. French merchants became very interested in the cultivation of groundnuts in Senegal. It was some such merchants who wanted to see effective direction of affairs in Senegal to promote their business interests who are said to have suggested the appointment of Faidherbe as governor of the colony.

Questions

1. Describe the emergence of Creole society.
2. Assess Creole achievement in general.
3. Show how the peoples outside the Colony of Sierra Leone were brought under the influence of the Colony.
4. Why and how was a 'Protectorate' declared over the hinterland of Sierra Leone?
5. Give reasons for the Creole decline.
6. Do you see any differences in Americo-Liberian and Creole societies?
7. Describe the achievements of Joseph Jenkins Roberts in Liberia.
8. What were the main difficulties in the attainment of national unity in Liberia?
9. Describe the economic situation in Liberia up to 1900.
10. Why was Liberia unable to become a clear symbol of independence to other parts of West Africa?
11. How established were the French in Senegal by 1850?
12. Describe how the French policy of assimilation worked in Senegal.
13. Assess the efforts of Faidherbe towards the establishment of French rule and general progress in Senegal.
14. What did Négritude stand for? Why was it less appealing in British West Africa?
15. What was the importance of groundnuts in the economic development of Senegal?

For further reading

Fyfe, C., *A Short History of Sierra Leone*, Longman, 1962.
Clarke, R., *Sierra Leone*, African Publication Society, (new impression) 1969.
Tarikh Vol. 1, No. 4, 1967 (pp. 43–54), Longman.
Crowder, M., *Senegal: A Study in French Assimilation Policy*, Faber and Faber, 1962.
Yancy, E. J., *The Republic of Liberia*, Allen and Unwin, 1959.

6 The Gold Coast in the nineteenth century

Asante and Fante

Origins of the Fante states

The Asante and Fante belong to the Akan or Twi-speaking peoples of the Gold Coast, modern Ghana. The Akan form by far the largest group, accounting for more than a half of the population of the country. After years of wandering southward from the vast grassland country to the north, the ancestors of the Akan made their first notable settlement in Ghana in the region of Takyiman, about a hundred miles north of the modern city of Kumasi. From Takyiman the ancestors of the Fante moved progressively farther south until they finally reached Fanteland, their present home to the west of what is today Greater Accra. It has not been possible to date with any degree of certainty the time when the Fante left Takyiman but as a matter of fact some Fante groups were already well settled on the coast when the Portuguese appeared in the Gold Coast towards the end of the fifteenth century.

The first major settlement of the Fante in their southern home was at Mankesim which still remains a sizeable town lying on the main road from Accra to Takoradi in the Western Region of Ghana. Mankesim in the Akan language really means *great or principal town*. From Mankesim splinter groups moved to the north, east, west and farther south until eventually the Fante came to occupy the large area that became Fanteland. The cause of the exodus from Mankesim is not known for certain, but it could well have been pressure of overpopulation and internal strife. In any case the Fante groups that moved out of Mankesim spread into country already inhabited by earlier peoples such as the Asebu, Aguafo, Fetu and Ahanta. In time the Fante and the earlier peoples were fused together and eventually several quite large Fante states were established. Although these Fante states managed to achieve some kind of overall union in the course of the eighteenth century this union was at its very best nothing like the closely-knit Asante union of the early eighteenth century and after. Fanteland never produced kings like Osei Tutu and Opoku Ware of Asante, nor was it blessed with a statesman and a genius like Okomfo Anokye. When one Fante state managed to attain a leading position in the loose union, it was at best only a senior among equals. Even in the face of external threats Fanteland remained, by and large, a scene of fragmented authority.

By the middle of the eighteenth century, about the time of the death of Opoku Ware of Asante, the worthy successor of Osei Tutu, the alignment of powerful states in the Gold Coast in relation to the Fante states was something like this. To the east of Fanteland were the Ga-Adangbe states. To the north of these states was Akyem Abuakwa which had lately overcome the once powerful Akwamu kingdom and caused the dismemberment of the Akwamu empire. Lying in between Asante and Fante were a number of states tributary to Asante such as Denkyira, Wassa and Assin. The overall position was that by 1750 nearly the whole of modern Ghana (both north and south) with the exception of Fante and some smaller states to the far west of the country, had fallen under Asante control or influence. The falling of Fante too under Asante domination appeared to be only a question of time and the Fante themselves sensed what was imminent.

Asante-Fante relations
The first major open conflict between Asante and Fante had occurred in 1765. The overthrow of the Denkyira yoke and the defeat of Akim by Asante in the early years of the eighteenth century had paved the way for increased trade between the Asante and the Europeans on the coast. The Europeans for their part welcomed this development. The Asante also attached great importance to the purchase of firearms from the Europeans. They needed ever greater quantities of guns and ammunition to keep their constant military campaigns going and also to hold the vast Asante empire together. However, the Asante always complained that the states through which Asante traders passed to reach the coast were unduly hostile. They also felt that the Fante middlemen through whom they transacted business with the Europeans often cheated them. In 1765 King Osei Kwadwo of Asante found it necessary to mount an attack against the Wassa for blocking the Asante trade routes to the coast. Things came to a head when the Wassa managed to draw the Denkyira, Twifo and Akim to their side and thus placed not only the Western Asante trade routes to Fanteland but also the eastern ones to the Accra area in danger. In the course of the Asante invasion of Wassa, Osei Kwadwo was able to persuade the Fante to join him against the Wassa and their allies. Wassa resistance quickly collapsed before the combined onslaught by Asante and Fante. This should have ended the

Asante incursion to the south and the Fante were anxious that the Asante army should leave the south and return home. However, the Asante did not leave. Osei Kwadwo indeed camped his army at Abora, a major Fante town not far from Cape Coast. This brought Asante arms right inside Fanteland. Provocative acts on both sides brought the uneasy alliance between Asante and Fante to an end and there finally developed an open confrontation between the former allies. The situation was, however, saved when Osei Kwadwo suddenly decided to take back his army to Asante. The next few years were, however, filled with fears and rumours of renewed Asante attack on the Fante. Nothing happened before Osei Kwadwo's death in 1781.

The British traders on the coast were thoroughly alarmed by the prospect of war between Asante and Fante. Such a war, they feared, would create chaos and adversely affect trade. For the rest of the century the British did all they could to dissuade Asante from attacking the Fante in particular or invading the south in general.

Renewal of hostilities

During the course of the nineteenth century the Asante and Fante were at war for no fewer than nine times. The nineteenth century wars should in reality be called Asante-Fante-British wars, for the British were more or less actively involved in nearly all of them. The most important of these wars, that of 1874, was British-led and was virtually a British invasion of Asante. This war is locally known as the 'Sargrenti' war after Sir Garnet Wolseley, the British commander. British involvement in the Asante–Fante conflct stemmed from committed British support to the Fante and other southern states. The position taken by the British has already been broadly outlined. A general state of chaos through warfare was not conducive to British trade. The British genuinely feared that if the Asante conquered the Fante and the other neighbouring states, trade in general would fall under Asante control. The Asante actually wanted peace. They wanted to ensure that their traders travelled to the coast and back without molestation. Trade with the Europeans on the coast was so vital to the Asante that they took special pains to cultivate friendly relations with Elmina in the west and Accra in the east. The ready acceptance by Elmina of Asante friendship and protection vexed the other Fante states.

During the first decade of the nineteenth century a major conflict occurred between Asante and Fante. The full story of this first clash between the two powers in the nineteenth century has already been told in detail in Book One. An Asante army followed two Assin fugitive chiefs who were running away from punishment by the Asantehene, their overlord. They entered Fanteland and finally sought and obtained refuge in the British fort at Anomabo. The British governor, urged by the Fante, refused to hand over the two Assin chiefs to the Asante. In the end the Asantehene Osei Bonsu himself appeared at the head of the Asante army which, after negotiations for the surrender of the fugitive chiefs had broken down, took the town of Anomabo and pressed on towards the British fort, to which many of the townsmen had fled for shelter. In the eyes of the Asante this successful invasion of Fanteland placed the Fante states under Asante domination. In future years the Asantehene was to regard the Fante chiefs as his subjects. However, neither the Fante nor their British protectors and friends were prepared to admit the Asante claim. This was to lead to a series of further conflicts in the course of the century.

Now that the Asante empire embraced nearly the whole of modern Ghana the Asante rightly hoped to reap the fruits of their conquest and labour. They expected to have greater freedom in trading with the Europeans on the coast. The Asantehene expected respect and obedience from the Fante chiefs. However, the attitude of the Fante and the British proved disappointing. Provocative acts by the Fante led to the next outbreak of war. The war in 1824 was more than an Asante-Fante war; it was an Asante-Fante-British war. Hostilities were touched off when Asante warriors were despatched to the coast to seize an Anomabo policeman alleged to have abused the Asantehene while engaged in a hot exchange of words with an Asante trader on the coast.

Three years earlier the British forts on the Gold Coast, the so-called British settlements, had been placed under the administration of the governor of Sierra Leone. The governor for the combined settlements, Sir Charles MacCarthy, arrived in the Gold Coast in 1822 when Asante-Fante relations were very bad. The Fante exaggerated the situation: they held up the Asante as greedy tyrants, and succeeded in working up MacCarthy to plan a punitive expedition against an Asante army camped below the river Pra in the south. The British merchants on the coast added their voice to that of the Fante chiefs in clamouring for war against Asante. They pointed out that if Asante was not overthrown or Asante power reduced, the British might as well withdraw from the country. MacCarthy was convinced and he decided to show the states of the coast that they were not without protection by the British. An expedition to the interior against the Asante was hastily planned. By the end of 1823 nearly all the Fante states, with the exception of Elmina, were up in arms against the Asante. The expedition, however, ended in utter disaster when the Asante army cut the allied forces to pieces at the Battle of Nsamankow. The governor, Sir Charles MacCarthy, was killed. The result of the war came as a rude shock to the British.

However, the British and their coastal allies did not have to wait for long to blot out the shame of 1824. In 1826 the Asante marched again to the south specifically to punish the Gas of Accra for abandoning their long-standing alliance with Asante. The importance of Accra and Elmina as faithful allies of the Asante has already been pointed out. An alliance of a motley group of coastal and southern states led by the British managed luckily to put an Asante army to confusion and retreat on the plains of Dodowa in Shai, some twenty miles north-east of Accra. This victory over Asante was followed by a treaty in 1831 when the Asante were made reluctantly to renounce their authority over their southern subject states of Akim, Wassa, Denkyira, Fante, Assin and Accra. This was a bitter pill for the Asante to swallow and they never reconciled themselves to the loss. However, for a quarter of a century an uneasy peace prevailed in southern Ghana. However, the Asante were all the time watching for an opportunity to make good their loss.

The British had now become very much involved in the conflicts between the Asante on one hand and the Fante and the other southern states on the other. From the position of an interested sympathizer, then to that of a not unbiased umpire trying to hold the balance between the Asante and the Fante, the British had now become virtually a leading partner in a coalition against Asante. In the course of the second half of the nineteenth century the southern states, including Fante, became a kind of unofficial British 'protectorate'.

In 1852 the spell of peace was disturbed when an Asante army crossed the River Pra into the south following more trouble with two Assin chiefs, subjects of the Asantehene. It turned out, however, to be a brief affair. The Asante army retired without fighting. However, this sudden disturbance of the peace led to fear and speculation among the British and their Fante allies.

In 1863 trouble with Asante again revived. It was once again over the old question of escaping refugees seeking protection on the coast. There were two cases. The first was a runaway boy, a slave; the second was an old man (not a slave) accused of keeping for himself a gold nugget instead of surrendering it to the Asantehene as the Asante maintained their laws said he should. The case was handled in an atmosphere of mistrust and misunderstanding. The British governor, Richard Pine, could have sent back the old man to Asante seeking assurance of his safety from the Asantehene. However, he regarded the Asantehene as a tyrant who might not keep his word. So Pine refused to send back the old man to Asante fearing that he would be killed the moment he arrived back in Asante. Matters soon got out of hand and the Asantehene, surprised at the behaviour of the British governor, sent down an army which soon crossed the Pra. The army only pillaged villages and returned to Asante but the short-lived invasion had far-reaching repercussions. A number of British troops were frantically dispatched to the Pra in case the Asante army returned to the attack. Some of the British troops died as the result of an outbreak of dysentery. The

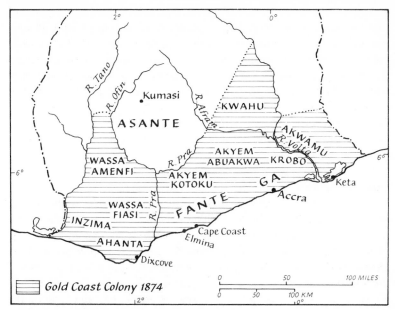

Gold Coast Colony, 1874

matter was mentioned in the British Parliament in London and the Government began to have second thoughts about its position in relation not only to the states on the Gold Coast but the British settlements in West Africa in general. A Select Committee of the British Parliament in 1865 actually recommended that the British should gradually quit their settlements in West Africa and turn over the administration to the Africans of these settlements. However, as we shall see later, the situation in the Gold Coast changed for the better within a few years and the British gave up the idea of leaving. It was in such circumstances that the 1874 war was carried into the capital of Asante by British and other troops from the southern states.

Once the British made up their mind not to quit the Gold Coast, as they had been considering for some time, it became their uppermost design to humiliate the Asante and remove their authority over the country as a whole. They saw in the removal of the Asante menace an opportunity for expansion of their economic activities even farther north beyond Asante. The troubles of the Asante invasion of 1863 had still not been resolved. In 1867, as we shall see later, an exchange of forts on the coast was arranged between the Dutch and the British. The Asante became alarmed over the possibility of losing their hold on Elmina. When in 1869 the Asante renewed their attack on the south the British decided to break Asante power once and for all. Sir Garnet

Wolseley, an eminent British soldier, arrived in the Gold Coast to plan the attack on Asante. In 1873 thorough preparations were made; every advantage was taken of the experience of the disaster of 1824. The Asante were beaten back from the Pra until Wolseley's forces finally entered a deserted Kumasi, parts of which were set on fire before the expedition retired. This was a most humiliating blow to the Asante and a turning point in the history of the Gold Coast. In the Treaty of Fomena, which followed their defeat, the Asante were compelled to renounce their authority over a number of southern states including Sefwi, Wassa, Assin, Denkyira, Fante, Kwahu, Akim and Accra.

Asante after 1874

The Treaty of Fomena and the resulting loss of a large part of the Asante empire was not the end of the troubles of Asante. The destruction of the military power and prestige of Asante in 1874 was a signal for the vassal states of Dagomba, Gonja, Gyaman and Krache to the north to declare their independence. There was thus after 1874 a total break-up of the once impressive Asante empire. Except for Brong-Ahafo only the original kindred states (metropolitan Asante) now acknowledged the authority of the Asantehene and the Golden Stool. The continued cohesion of the metropolitan areas has been pointed out as a testimony of the nation-building capacity of Osei Tutu and Okomfo Anokye.

However, even inside metropolitan Asante trouble occurred soon after the disastrous events of 1874. A civil war broke out between Kumasi and Juaben. As a result of this there was a mass movement of the people of Juaben to Koforidua in the south where they eventually established the state of New Juaben. Then in the early 1880s Kokofu, Mampong and Nsuta, all original members of the Asante union, rebelled. This was a most trying period in the history of Asante.

What was the attitude of the British to the internal difficulties of Asante? There is ample evidence to show that the British not only took satisfaction in the trying conflicts within Asante but also actually intrigued with some of the rebellious states for the ultimate dismemberment of the Asante nation.

When in 1880 Kwaku Dua III (better known as Prempeh I) ascended the Golden Stool, there were soon hopeful signs that Asante might overcome its internal troubles and even retrieve some of the losses after 1874. The new Asantehene skilfully negotiated an end to the rebellion by Kokofu, Mampong and Msuta. He even tried to get the Juabens who had moved to the south to return. If only Prempeh I had been left alone there was great promise that he could have restored Asante's position considerably. However, his reign fell within the dark period of intensive scramble for colonies by the European powers in West Africa. The British, who had by the 1880s consolidated their position in the south of the Gold Coast, were anxious to get hold of Asante too before the French in the Ivory Coast could steal a march on them. They were determined to thwart Prempeh I's efforts to reconstruct the Asante nation. In 1891 they offered their protection to Asante but Prempeh I politely but firmly refused the offer. This did not save him nor his nation. In 1896 Asante was surprised and tricked by a British-led military expedition to Kumasi. Prempeh I was seized and taken to the coast and finally deported to the Seychelles Islands in the Indian Ocean off the East African coast. Asante was then annexed by the British.

Growth of British Rule

At the beginning of the nineteenth century the main British forts on the Gold Coast were those at Cape Coast, Accra and Anomabo. There were lesser ones at Dixcove, Winneba, Tantum, Komenda and Prampram. These forts and limited areas of land around them constituted what were known as the British settlements in the Gold Coast. The British subjects in the country were strictly speaking the British merchants, regular troops in the forts, and a few Africans working in the forts. What was termed British territory was thus quite negligible and the population of British subjects was very tiny.

Until 1821 the affairs of the British settlements had been managed by a Committee of Merchants representing the British trading interests known as the Company of Merchants. After the Act of Abolition of 1807 the British Government began to doubt if the merchants so steeped in the slave trade were the right people to manage the affairs of the British settlements. It is to be noted that the British merchants in the Gold Coast had petitioned the British Government to grant them a period of grace before attacking the slave trade seriously so that they could adjust their trade and finances. The British Government did not feel much impressed by the petition.

After the first decade of the nineteenth century the British Government was not at all sure what it wanted to do about the settlements on the Gold Coast. The troubles following the Asante invasion of the coast in 1807 coupled with the unprofitable nature of trade in the Gold Coast raised doubts about the wisdom in the British Government continuing to make grants towards the maintenance of the forts. After a series of investigations, however, it was recommended that the Government should not withdraw its support of and interest in the forts. It was finally decided in 1821 that the African Company should be abolished and the settlements placed directly under the British Crown. The settlements in the Gold Coast were to be annexed to those in Sierra Leone. Sir Charles MacCarthy, governor of Sierra Leone, about whom we have heard already, was given responsibility for the settlements in the Gold Coast.

The total failure of MacCarthy's expedition against the Asante in 1824 proved a shock to the British Government. The decision to take over the settlements in the Gold Coast by the Crown was regretted. Evacuation was contemplated but it was considered shameful and embarrassing to quit in circumstances of British military defeat. However, after the Asante had been defeated two years later in 1826 at Dodowa it was thought that the time had come for the British to withdraw honourably. Plans were accordingly made and in 1828 the administration of the British forts in the Gold Coast was turned over to a Committee of Merchants in London through an appointed Council of Merchants drawn from British traders living on the Gold Coast. Up to the end of 1829 the Council had an acting President in the person of John Jackson, the most senior British resident merchant on the coast. In January 1830 Captain George Maclean, a naval officer with considerable experience in West Africa, became full President of the Council of Merchants. Maclean was not a governor directly representing the British Crown; he was an agent of the Committee of Merchants. The British Government was, however, interested in the administration of the Council of Merchants as it made a yearly grant for running the forts. Maclean remained at his post till 1843. Those thirteen years under his administration were most important for the development of British rule in the Gold Coast.

Maclean's administration (1830–43)

When the Council of Merchants began its work the British Government told it in clear terms that its jurisdiction was to be limited to the British forts. However, the Council, both during the short time that John Jackson acted as its President as well as during the thirteen years under Maclean, found it difficult and impracticable to keep strictly to its instructions. Before Maclean became its President the Council did take notice of what was happening outside the forts. It found it necessary to reprimand Chief Aggrey of Cape Coast for hoisting in front of his house a flag with a picture of the Asantehene kneeling before him, Aggrey. The Council thought that Chief Aggrey's action was dangerously provocative and might offer an excuse for an Asante invasion. The Council went further: it sought to establish a medium of communication with Asante by offering a reward for a messenger who would carry a letter to the Asantehene in Kumasi.

Maclean took up the question of relations with Asante seriously. In 1831 he was finally able to conclude a peace treaty with Asante. By the terms of this treaty the Asantehene agreed to recognize the independence of Denkyira, Assin, Twifu, Fante, Nzima and other former vassal states to Asante in the south. The Asantehene also agreed to submit any disputes between himself and the states in the south to Maclean and his Council for peaceful settlement. Surprisingly too the Asantehene agreed further to

George Maclean

deposit 600 ounces of gold in the Cape Coast Castle and to send two Asante royals to Cape Coast, virtually as hostages, in earnest of his desire for peace. On their part the states in the south were to keep all trade paths including those from Asante to the coast open and safe for all. The treaty was a great diplomatic victory for Maclean. It helped to ensure peace in the sense that while it gave the southern states their independence it also guaranteed to the Asante security of their trade with the Europeans on the coast.

Gradually and skilfully Maclean imposed British jurisdiction over a large area in the southern areas of the Gold Coast. In 1832 it was reported to Maclean and the Council that murder and other acts of atrocity had been committed near Cape Coast. The criminal was apprehended and brought before the Council, which was aware that, technically, it had no authority over such cases. However, Maclean assembled the chiefs of Cape Coast and asked them to try the criminal by their own laws, but the Council was to see that the criminal, if found guilty, was not tortured. The Council thus widened the scope of its judicial functions. In 1836 it decided that criminals in the neighbouring states should be tried by their own local authorities, but the President and the Council were to see that no injustice was done and that opportunity was given to prisoners to defend themselves and that general fairness was upheld. From this position the Council finally took upon itself the enforcement of law and order in the nearby states. Kwadwo Tsiboe,

Chief of Denkyira, who was alleged to have indulged in human sacrifice while celebrating the funeral of his mother, was summoned before the Council in Cape Coast and was made to pay a fine. In 1834 Maclean had taken an even bolder step. He ordered a military action against an Nzima Chief of Apolonia, said to have sold some of his own subjects to a Spanish trader. The chief was ordered to deposit 300 ounces of gold in Cape Coast against his future good behaviour. He promised good treatment of his subjects and undertook in future to refer cases involving the death penalty to the Council in Cape Coast.

In such ways Maclean extended the idea of British justice and the jurisdiction of the Council of Merchants to a wide area in southern Gold Coast. This jurisdiction had no legal basis and was in fact against the British Government's instructions to the Council. However, the essential fairness of Maclean's jurisdiction won the approval of the neighbouring states. The local chiefs brought cases on their own free will to Maclean to try. Gradually an unofficial British 'Protectorate' developed in southern Gold Coast spreading some 150 miles along the coast and 80 miles inland. The fairness of Maclean's judgments and his commanding personality inspired confidence in his administration throughout the 'Protectorate'. Even the Asante had great respect for Maclean. His death in 1847 was deeply mourned in Asante. So committed was he to peace and order in the 'Protectorate' that in the later years of his administration Maclean stationed soldiers in all important towns within the 'Protectorate' who conveyed his messages to the local chiefs and reported back to him what was happening in the various states. Maclean's authority rested largely on the goodwill of the local chiefs and their peoples.

The very success and nature of Maclean's administration caused misgivings about the status of the 'Protectorate'. His foes, some lesser British residents on the coast, began to spread vicious rumours about him. He was, for example, accused of condoning slavery. Maclean was always faced with the question of domestic slavery which was an institution deep-rooted in the states of the Gold Coast. Domestic slaves were, as a rule, treated on almost equal terms with members of the families in which they served. They could acquire property of their own, and even inherit the property of their masters. Some domestic slaves could rise to positions of distinction in society. However, their status was essentially that of slaves all the same, and this fact, coupled with possible abuses of the system, made it intolerable to the the British sense of freedom of the individual. It is true that the system was liable to abuse but Maclean realized that its abuses could be mitigated, and in any case it was too deep-rooted to be abolished outright. He knew too well that without its tacit recognition it would have been impossible to exercise any influence on the peoples and their chiefs.

In 1841 a Dr Madden was commissioned to visit the Gold Coast to inquire into Maclean's administration. He appears to have been prejudiced against Maclean right from the start of his assignment. After his inquiries he observed that the British authorities in the Gold Coast had no right to try and punish local Africans on behalf of their chiefs. Maclean himself would admit that his jurisdiction had no legal sanction; but he had taken the practical view that this jurisdiction conferred benefits upon the Africans within the 'Protectorate'. The British Government, suspicious about Madden's openly unfavourable report on Maclean's administration, asked a Select Committee to review the report. The Committee's final observations run as follows:

'We fully admit the merits of that administration, whether we look to the officer employed, Captain Maclean, or the Committee under whom he has acted, which . . . has exercised from the four ill-provided forts of Dixcove, Cape Coast, Anomabo and British Accra . . . a very wholesome influence over a coast not much less than 150 miles in extent and to a considerable distance inland; preventing within that range external Slave Trade, maintaining peace and security, and exercising a useful, though irregular jurisdiction among neighbouring tribes.'

The Committee, however, recommended that the British Crown should assume direct responsibility for the settlements. Subsequently in 1843 the British Government assumed direct responsibility for the British forts and settlements on the Gold Coast. Commander Hill was appointed Governor while Maclean was given the new post of Judicial Assessor. One of the first acts of the new Governor was to take advantage of courtesy calls made on him by groups of chiefs from the Protectorate to sign a series of treaties collectively known as the Bond of 1844.

It was once considered that the Bond of 1844 marked the beginning of real British rule in the Gold Coast. In actual fact it did not. What the Bond was meant to do was to give a legal basis to, and so regularize, Maclean's administration; in other words, to give official recognition to the Protectorate. The Bond introduced practically nothing new into the administration that followed. Unfortunately, Commander Hill and the governors who succeeded him did not command the same influence over the states in the Protectorate as Maclean had done. Maclean himself, as Judical Assessor, lamented the fact that he no longer possessed enough authority to deal with difficult situations. In 1846 when there were fears of an Asante invasion of the coast Maclean noted in a private correspondence: 'Three years ago I would with the power and influence which I then wielded have set matters right again in ten days'.

Maclean died in May 1847 and so passed away one of the ablest British administrators in the Gold Coast. He did more than anyone else to lay the foundation of British rule in the country.

After Maclean

From the end of Maclean's administration to about 1873 the British Government was constantly groping for a policy in the Gold Coast. We can only touch on a few salient points in the developments during this period.

Two important developments took place in the Gold Coast in 1850. In January the Gold Coast was separated from Sierra Leone and given its own government. The governor was to be assisted by an executive as well as a legislative council. Then in March the Danes decided to quit the Gold Coast and they sold their forts to the east of Accra to the British for £10,000. The Danes had established a kind of protectorate over Akwapim and Akim. Danish influence in the two states now passed on to the British.

The British Government was willing to establish social services (such as schools, hospitals and roads) in the 'Protectorate' but it had no funds to do this. Although the British now controlled the coast east of Accra with the departure of the Danes, trade was sluggish in the area and there were no prospects of collecting customs and duties on trade. The chiefs and their peoples were eager for social development. It was decided that the people should pay for such development. In April 1852 a gathering of chiefs and elders from various parts of the 'Protectorate' took place in Cape Coast in the presence of the governor. It was decided that a poll tax of one shilling a head for every man, woman and child should be levied. The gathering constituted itself into a legislative assembly and claimed that it could make laws for the 'Protectorate'.

The Poll Tax was not a success. It was not popular and led to riots in a few areas on the coast near Accra. The little money that was collected nearly all went in paying the collectors.

The later 1850s and the earlier 1860s witnessed renewed troubles between Asante and the British and the states in the south. After the brief Asante invasion of 1863 and the loss of British lives when a contingent of British troops was rushed to the Pra, the whole question of whether Britain should continue to have responsibility not only for the settlements in the Gold Coast but also for the others throughout West Africa came to the forefront. In 1865 a Select Committee of the British Parliament was appointed to study the question and make recommendations to the British Government. The Committee's final recommendation was that the British should withdraw from West Africa, but to avoid chaos resulting, the withdrawal should be gradual while the Africans were quickly made to accept full responsibility for their own affairs. Some educated Fante began to persuade their chiefs and people to think of organizing a government which would be able to take over when the British should leave the Gold Coast. However, the day for the departure of the British never came.

In 1867 an alarming situation arose in the Gold Coast; to be precise in the coastal Fante areas. For many years the situation in which British and Dutch settlements were interlocked on the coast had been a principal source of weakness to the British administration. The situation made it impossible for the British to collect adequate revenue through the imposition of duties as the Dutch were not inclined to do the same. To have imposed duties in the British settlements alone would have meant driving out trade into the Dutch settlements. In 1867, however, an exchange of forts was arranged which put the Dutch on one side and the British on the other of the coast. Serious trouble attended the execution of this arrangement. The people of Komenda refused to allow the Dutch to occupy the British fort there and even began to attack the people of Elmina. The Dutch decided amidst the general chaos to pull out of the Gold Coast altogether, offering to sell their forts and possessions in the country to the British. The idea was naturally pleasing to the British who now saw the prospect of being in full control of the entire coastline. They could now collect revenue to pay for their administration by imposing duties on trade. So the 1865 Select Committee's idea of withdrawal was quickly dropped.

When the troubles over the transfer of forts started a number of Fante chiefs met at Mankesim and agreed to help the people of Komenda against Elmina. The meeting of the Fante chiefs quickly developed into a kind of Confederation. By the end of 1870 the Confederation had become a great political movement in which the chiefs were ably supported and directed by educated elements. In 1871 a carefully worded written constitution was produced for the Confederation. The constitution sought to create friendship and co-operation among the various Fante chiefs. It made provision for the building of roads and schools. It further sought to improve agriculture and to exploit the mineral resources of the area. There was to be a Confederacy Government with a General Assembly of elected members, both chiefs and non-chiefs. The Assembly would have power to make laws and to levy taxes. In short the constitution was a preparation towards Fante independence. Such a development might have been tolerable at the time of the Select Committee's recommendations in 1865 or at least before the exchange of forts. However, in 1870, with the departure of the Dutch, the British were in no mood for such a development. The leaders of the Confederation were arrested and locked up by the British authorities in the Gold Coast. These leaders were said to be a small clique of agitators and discontented elements who wanted power for themselves. In fact the makers of the Constitution had requested the recognition, advice and support of the British Government in order to make it work successfully. Indeed they received a rude shock. Although they were later released on the orders of the British Colonial Office in London, the death of the Confederation was certain. And thus a laudable attempt to combine traditional and European ideas of government was lost and the way was made clear for the effective establishment of British rule in the Gold Coast.

It was in such circumstances that Asante power was broken by the expedition of 1874. The capital of the Gold Coast Colony was removed from Cape Coast to Accra in that year. We have already seen how the British attitude towards Asante finally resulted in the humiliating deportation of Prempeh I which left the Asante nation without a head. In 1900 a British Governor visited Kumasi, the capital of Asante, and asked that the Golden Stool be fetched for him to sit on as a representative of the British monarch. This rash demand sparked off an Asante revolt which was eventually suppressed in 1901. Asante was then annexed by the British Crown. About the same time the British led expeditions into the hinterland of Asante, ostensibly to check slave raiding activities, and a series of treaties with local rulers ended in a British Protectorate being proclaimed over what for a long time remained the Northern Territories, now the Northern and Upper Regions of Ghana. Thus by the early years of the present century British rule had spread over the whole of modern Ghana except the eastern section, now called the Volta Region, where the Germans had forestalled the British and which they had annexed as part of German Togoland.

Questions

1. Show how the Fante established themselves in their present homeland.
2. What were the main causes of friction and conflict between Asante and Fante?
3. Why and how did the British become involved in the conflicts between Asante and the states of the south of the Gold Coast?
4. Why did the British Government hand over the administration of the British settlements on the Gold Coast to the Council of Merchants?
5. Describe the aims and methods of George Maclean's administration on the Gold Coast.
6. Why did the British Government resume administration of the Gold Coast in 1843?
7. What is the significance of the so-called Bond of 1844?
8. Give reasons for the ultimate failure of the Mankesim Constitutional proposals?
9. Explain why the British attacked Asante in 1874 and in 1896.

For further reading

Metcalf, G. E., *Great Britain and Ghana*, Thomas Nelson and Sons, 1964.
Metcalfe, G. E., *Maclean of the Gold Coast*, Oxford University Press, 1962.
Ward, W. E. F., *A History of Ghana*, Allen and Unwin, 1952.

7 Dahomey, Oyo and Benin in the nineteenth century

Dahomey

Dahomey, as we saw in Book One, began as a small kingdom belonging to a family of states of the kindred peoples known as the Aja. It was first established on the central plateau of the modern West African state that still bears the name Dahomey, with Abomey, some fifty miles away from the coast, as its chief town. It later conquered the more important and senior Aja states of Allada and Whydah in 1724 and 1727 respectively. By the end of the eighteenth century the kingdom had won a considerable reputation for the efficiency of its internal political organization. It had developed a system of government surprisingly modern in nature and quite in advance of that of many other states in West Africa. It had evolved an effective system of taxation, although it was not always rich, and it enjoyed a reasonably good system of communication. The king obtained minute details of the wealth of districts, towns and villages. The kingdom had departments of government each with clearly defined responsibilities and headed by reliable state officials. In later years Dahomey was to embark upon the development of state-owned plantations of oil palm as a measure to diversify the economy of the state. All this should be to the lasting credit of Dahomey as a West African state. However, it seems that certain aspects of the power and position of Dahomey have tended to be exaggerated. To correct the impression created as a result of this tendency it may be useful for us, before starting to discuss the fortunes of the kingdom in the nineteenth century (which is what this part of the chapter is mainly about), to examine some of the doubtful notions popularly held about Dahomey.

Most important of all, perhaps, it may be pointed out that the military strength of Dahomey in general has been over-estimated. The usual story is that the Dahomean army was invincible and constituted a terror to all the neighbours of the kingdom. This impression is in fact not borne out by available evidence. It is true that the Dahomean soldiers were carefully drilled and that the eye-witness accounts by those who saw them on parade have nothing but praise for their impressive turn-out. The Dahomean army as a whole was led by quite worthy generals and captains. However, the fact still remains that the record of its various campaigns shows that it suffered many defeats and won few victories. Nearly always when it encountered the Oyo army on the battlefield the Dahomean army broke up in confusion.

Before its conquest by Dahomey in 1724 the Aja state of Allada had been a kind of dependency of Oyo. For this reason Oyo reacted sharply to the attack on that state by Dahomey. Between 1726 and 1730 Oyo invaded Dahomey no fewer than four times. In 1730 an Oyo army entered the Dahomean capital of Abomey and occupied it for some time. Agadja, the Dahomean king (1708–40) had to accept a tributary position for his kingdom and for the next hundred years Dahomey remained within the Oyo empire. King Agadja and his successors made repeated attempts to shake off the yoke of Oyo, but Dahomey was on each occasion beaten and put back in its place.

The yoke of Oyo was a distasteful humiliation for Dahomey. Apart from the considerable yearly tribute that Dahomey paid to Oyo, the domination by Oyo hurt in apparently small things. For example, a particularly humiliating experience for the king of Dahomey was the fact that he was not to wear garments made of certain materials used by his over-lord, the Alafin or King of Oyo.

The hold that Oyo exercised over Dahomey, however, proved beneficial in certain respects. Dahomey was compelled to remain at peace with its neighbours and was thus saved from wasting her limited resources on fruitless wars. It was, moreover, protected from attack by others for it was clear that Oyo would punish whoever ventured to attack Dahomey. The resulting peace that Dahomey enjoyed must have helped it to develop its internal organization. Furthermore, there is evidence that Oyo culture influenced Dahomey in various ways, especially in religious beliefs and administrative ideas. These developments were never acknowledged by the Dahomeans, nor did they mitigate the Dahomean dislike of Oyo domination.

There are other untrue notions about Dahomey besides the exaggerated military strength and position of the kingdom. Travellers' tales portray the Dahomeans as a blood-thirsty people and their king as a violent tyrant. However, in reality the Dahomeans were no less hospitable than other West African peoples in spite of the fact that Europeans visiting Abomey were sometimes delayed unduly and subjected to other kinds of inconvenience. Visitors invited to witness important state ceremonies, on seeing signs of human sacrifice, were apt to conclude that human life was of little value to the Dahomeans. It may be observed that during the nineteenth century at least, royal officials probed into the sudden deaths even of slaves employed on plantations and in Dahomean homes to ensure that there had been no foul play.

While his authority was generally undisputed and his person sometimes treated with exaggerated respect by his subjects, the Dahomean king was not free to do what he pleased. There were checks and balances to his power and quite often he went out of his way to please his subjects and to make concessions to them. The Dahomean monarchy was governed by customary constitution and by the dictates of ordinary common-sense. It appears to be the case that both in the grassland country to the north and in the forest of the south, the authority of the kings and rulers of West Africa was far from being unlimited. Dahomey was no exception to this.

Economic problems

During the eighteenth and nineteenth centuries the kings of Dahomey were continually faced with a serious economic situation. Whenever the economy became very bad a certain amount of political restlessness and instability became noticeable in the kingdom. So the kings had to do something about the economy of the state to keep their stool. For nearly two hundred years the slave trade remained the chief basis of the Dahomean economy. During

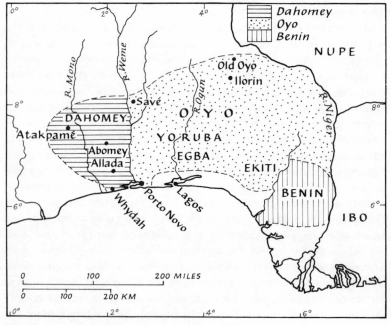

The Kingdoms of Dahomey, Oyo and Benin, c. 1800

the early years of the eighteenth century, however, King Agadja had ironically shown lack of sympathy and even positive hostility to the European slave trade. However, in about 1740 Dahomey became involved in the trade and appears for the next few years to have made a good business of it. From about the middle of the century, however, the prospects of the slave trade were not always certain. This uncertainty and the economic difficulties it created may be attributed to four factors.

Firstly, the Dahomean army was unable to procure a constant stream of captives to feed the slave markets on the coast so as to bolster the economy of the state. We have already noticed the general disability of the Dahomean army in the face of the watchful hold that the Oyo army maintained over Dahomey. The only area open to the Dahomean army for slave raids was the country to the north of the kingdom. However, the raids attempted by the Dahomean army in this direction did not always meet with success. King Kpengla (1774–89) is said to have sent out numerous slave-raiding expeditions to procure the slaves he badly needed to sell to the Europeans on the coast, but we are told that they 'were almost regularly defeated, sometimes disastrously'.

Secondly, the Oyo, who had steady supplies of slaves to sell, thanks to their numerous successful raids and wars, refused to sell their slaves at Dahomean ports. This deprived the King of Dahomey of substantial revenue he would have collected from the sale of these slaves. The Oyo kept under their control the marketing facilities at Porto Novo which was the capital of a small Oyo dependency called Ajase Ipo.

Thirdly, the period after the middle of the eighteenth century was not a good one for the slave trade in West Africa in general, and Dahomey was consequently severely hit. This period saw the chief slave-buying European nations notably England and France frequently at war with each other. This situation seriously disrupted the slave trade in West Africa. The result was that Dahomey was unable to find a ready and profitable market for even the limited number of slaves it could manage to procure.

Lastly, and the worst blow of all, came the abolition of the slave trade by Britain in 1807. The British then abandoned their slave depot at Whydah. The slave trade continued for years after the abolition, but when the British squadron obtained the right to search slave ships in the Gulf of Guinea and on the Atlantic in general, the economy of Dahomey fell on very bad days indeed.

Dahomey then tried to adjust itself to the changing situation. It began to develop an alternative basis for its economy. The Dahomean kings began to experiment with the cultivation of large oil palm plantations chiefly with slave labour. In fact royal plantations had been started as early as 1775. The difficult economic situation in the first half of the twentieth century encouraged the cultivation of more and more state-owned plantations. Plantations did not give quick money as the selling of slaves would. However, gradually oil replaced slaves as the mainstay of the Dahomean economy. It has been estimated that during the 1870s Dahomey was making as much as £500,000 annually through the sale of oil. Even so, the oil economy had its own difficulties for Dahomey. There were richer oil palm belts elsewhere in West Africa, notably in Yorubaland and in the Niger delta area.

Shaking off Oyo domination

For nearly a century Dahomey suffered irksome domination by Oyo. Time and again Dahomey had tried to end this domination through force of arms or refusal to pay the yearly tribute, but had only succeeded in bringing more punishment on itself. Between 1738 and 1748 King Tegbesu, who had succeeded Agadja, made futile attempts to end Oyo domination. After this failure Dahomey appears to have dutifully paid the yearly tribute until the end of the century. During the nineteenth century, however, Dahomey was at last able to turn the scales against Oyo.

Gezo (1818–58) and his successor Gelele (1858–89) were among the most outstanding rulers of Dahomey. The reign of the former coincided with a period of decline and grave difficulties for Oyo. Until the accession of Gezo things had not been going well for Dahomey itself. Frustration from the long period of Oyo domination as well as a serious economic depression had led to general dissatisfaction among Dahomeans towards the monarchy. In the midst of this situation King Agonglo was murdered in 1797. Confusion and uncertainty continued till 1818 when Gezo became king after overthrowing Adandozen, Agonglo's son and successor.

Gezo was a man of great political ability and action. His first goal was to achieve independence for Dahomey by bringing Oyo domination to an end. He also aimed at repairing the Dahomean economy. He was ably supported by a wealthy Portuguese mulatto trader at Whydah called da Souza. The opportunity was favourable for Gezo's plans against Oyo, for Oyo was by this time passing through serious internal troubles eventually leading to the final collapse of the Oyo empire.

After the death of the Alafin Abiodun in 1789 the central authority of Oyo had become progressively weaker. Things began to fall apart in the Oyo empire almost immediately after Abiodun's death. In 1793 there occurred a serious mutiny by a section of the Oyo army and many supporters of Alafin Awole were massacred. The Alafin himself was later compelled to commit suicide. His two immediate successors were also forced to commit suicide within less than a year of Awole's own death. Oyo was therefore left without central direction and authority. Indeed for several years there was no Alafin in Oyo. We shall examine the main causes for this confused situation later on, for our immediate concern is how Dahomey exploited this situation. In about 1817, Oyo was plunged into a serious civil war. King Gezo of Dahomey took advantage of the plight of Oyo and refused to pay tribute to her. Oyo must have been too pre-occupied with the civil war to worry about punishing Gezo for his action. Dahomey was thus left to regain its independence.

Soon after regaining its independence Dahomey found itself at loggerheads with another section of the Yoruba, the Egba. As a result of the general upheaval in Yorubaland the Egba had been forced to leave their original home to found a new home in Abeokuta in 1830. Dahomey must have felt uneasy about the establishment of a strong Egba centre at Abeokuta. Here was a possible rival state situated in a rich area of Yorubaland in which Dahomey was interested for expansion for both political and economic reasons. Gezo decided to move against Abeokuta before the city became too strong. He began by attacking some smaller settlements with which the Egba of Abeokuta had relations. During one of these attacks the Dahomean army was defeated and some important items of the royal regalia of Dahomey were captured. Recovery of the items gave Gezo added reason for attacking Abeokuta. In 1851 a Dahomean attack was made on Abeokuta but the Dahomeans were repulsed with heavy losses to themselves. Gezo was unable to avenge himself and make good the humiliation suffered by the Dahomeans before his death in 1858.

Gelele, Gezo's son, who succeeded him, swore to avenge his father's humiliating defeat by bringing Abeokuta to its knees. However, when he attacked the city in 1864 he suffered worse defeat than that of his father in 1851. Dahomey had to give up the idea of subduing Abeokuta and the Dahomean army contented itself with pillaging unprotected villages near Abeokuta by means of surprise attacks. The important thing was that Dahomey had been able to throw off the Oyo yoke as a result of the upheaval in Yorubaland.

Dahomey and France

In spite of vigorous attempts to revive the Dahomean economy, largely through the cultivation of oil palm plantations, neither Gezo nor Gelele was able to raise enough revenue to meet Dahomey's needs. Thus during the last two decades of the nineteenth century, when European powers were very swiftly carving out colonies for themselves in West Africa, Dahomey was caught poor and weak. By the end of the century France had annexed the kingdom of Dahomey which, together with neighbouring territories, became the French Colony of Dahomey, today the independent Republic of Dahomey.

French nationals had been trading on the so-called Slave Coast for many years. The fortunes of French traders on the Guinea Coast had changed from time to time with the fortunes of France itself in Europe during the nineteenth century. France, starting rather late, entered the colonial race in West Africa with redoubled energy. In 1878 Cotonou, a growing trade post on the coast, was ceded to France. In 1882 a French protectorate was declared over Porto Novo. By 1885 the entire coastal strip from Porto Novo westward to Anecho, in the modern Republic of Togo, had become effectively occupied by France. However, the kingdom of Dahomey regarded these coastal areas as under it or belonging to it. The French action was, therefore, viewed with alarm in Dahomey. Both Gelele and his successor Behanzin (1894) protested against France's intrusion. France, however, appears to have determined to take over the kingdom of Dahomey before the British or the Germans should move in and annex it. In 1889 the French sent a mission to the Dahomean capital of Abomey, demanding that Dahomey should end its pretensions to Cotonou. Afraid and confused, King Gelele died suddenly: he is believed to have committed suicide. Behanzin, Gelele's son, who succeeded him, was determined to resist the French demand. War eventually broke out between the Dahomeans and French forces. In November 1892 French troops entered Abomey. Behanzin was captured and exiled to the West Indies. The French created their own nominee, Agoliagbo, as King of Dahomey (1894–1900). Dahomey was at first placed under French protection but it eventually became a formal French colony. Thus ended the independence of one of the best organized states of West Africa.

The Oyo Kingdom of Yoruba

The kingdom of Oyo, established probably during the fifteenth century, had by the eighteenth century clearly distinguished itself as the leading state of the Yoruba-speaking peoples. It controlled an empire as extensive as any other in West Africa at the time. The kingdom appears to have reached the peak of its power and wealth during the reign of Abiodun (1785?–9). The Oyo empire then stretched in the north from the Niger, westward to the modern Republic of Dahomey and beyond. It is even believed that the western frontiers of the Oyo empire met the eastern limits of the Asante empire. From Nupe in the north the Oyo empire extended directly down to the edge of the forest belt. The capital of the kingdom was Old Oyo (until 1837) situated north of the modern town of Oyo. In the heart of Yorubaland in general was what has been called Metropolitan Oyo or Yoruba Proper: the area over which the effective authority of the Alafin of Oyo is believed to have evenly prevailed. The other parts of the empire enjoyed varying degrees of autonomy, some only paying tribute to the Alafin or performing periodic customs and ceremonies to mark their acceptance of him as overlord.

From the capital of Old Oyo, Alafin Abiodun secured Oyo trade routes to the coast with access to the ports of Little Ardra (later Porto Novo) and Badagry in the direction of Lagos. A steady flow of trade (mainly in slaves from the Oyo side) between Oyo and the coast led to increased revenue for the kingdom. Rev. Samuel Johnson, whose writings have contributed greatly to what is known of the modern history of the Yoruba, sees the reign of Abiodun as marking the end of an epoch in the history of the Yoruba. He writes:

'He [Abiodun] was the last of the kings who held the different parts of the kingdom together in one universal sway and with him ended the tranquillity and prosperity of the Yoruba country.'

Except through a dramatic military disaster or extraordinary national calamity kingdoms and empires do not fall abruptly without warning signs. The fall of a kingdom or empire is generally preceded by a period of decline. Even during the great period of Abiodun's reign the seeds of decline may be said to be already discernible in Oyo. The checks and balances to the constitutional authority in the kingdom had gradually created a situation in which only an Alafin of exceptional personality could keep his own position and prevent things from falling apart. Of special significance in the Oyo system of checks and balances was the position of the Oyo Mesi, the Council of State, whose powers often conflicted with the authority of the Alafin. The leader of this Council was the Basorum, a kind of prime minister in modern terminology. A strong Basorum could seek to dominate the Alafin and make it difficult, if not impossible, for him to rule. He could even cause the Alafin's death by calling upon him in the name of the Oyo Mesi and indeed of the people to commit suicide. A number of Alafins came to an untimely end in this way.

Abiodun had a dangerous Basorum called Gaha to deal with. However, he was able to strike first and secure himself by causing Gaha as well as his kinsmen in line of succession as Basorum to be slain. After getting rid of Gaha in this way Abiodun was able to place the Oyo Mesi under his control. However, although the members of the Oyo Mesi and other state office holders accepted the fact of Abiodun's ascendency they chafed under the Alafin's authority all the time and if a weaker person should become Alafin the familiar trouble was likely to start all over again. This was exactly what happened after Abiodun's death.

The start of open trouble

Awole, the man chosen to succeed Abiodun as Alafin, was not of a strong personality and trouble began at once with his reign. The commander-in-chief of the Oyo armies was known by the title Kakanfo. Next to the Basorum the Kakanfo was probably the most influential office-holder in the kingdom. It fell to the new Alafin to appoint a new Kakanfo. Traditionally the office was not to be held by a person of royal blood, but Awole ignored this and appointed a kinsman of his called Afonja to fill the post. Afonja was an ambitious man who had his eyes on the throne of the Alafin. He quickly began to build up his own power and forces to achieve his ambition. When Awole became aware of Afonja's designs, he sent him on a hazardous military campaign from which the Kakanfo was unlikely to return victorious. Awole thus hoped to get rid of Afonja quietly, for custom required a Kakanfo who lost an important battle not to return to Oyo but to commit suicide. However, things did not work out as Awole had hoped. Instead there occurred a mutiny in the Oyo army before the projected campaign could get under way. Soldiers known to be personally close and loyal to the Alafin were massacred almost to a man. After this shocking incident the Basorum demanded that the Alafin should commit suicide. This Awole did by taking poison. Two successive Alafins were similarly forced to commit suicide within a year of Awole's death. The central authority in Oyo was in this way seriously undermined and before long the kingdom was plagued by one disaster after another. The next half century or so witnessed a general state of confusion and progressive decline not only for Oyo but also for Yoruba as a whole.

Meanwhile the Kakanfo Afonja, who had become governor of the northern Oyo province of Ilorin, decided to assert his independence of the Alafin altogether. This incidentally was the period of dan Fodio's jihad which was gradually spreading from the north towards the south. To achieve the independence he wanted Afonja allied himself with a Fulani disciple of dan Fodio's called Mallam Alimi. With the support of Fulani mercenaries under the Mallam, Afonja was able to declare Ilorin independent of Oyo. But Afonja was playing with fire. In about 1824 the eldest son of Alimi, called Abdussalami, declared himself the ruler of Ilorin. Afonja was killed while trying to fight back for the control of Ilorin against Abdussalami. From Ilorin the Fulani began to push southward in a series of military campaigns that threatened Oyo. After a futile struggle to dislodge the Fulani from Ilorin, Oyo suffered a great humiliation when the Fulani entered the capital of Old Oyo and the Alafin offered to pay tribute to them.

Before committing suicide the Alafin Awole is said to have cursed Oyo in rather prophetic terms. He is reported to have said:

'My curse be upon you for your disloyalty and disobedience; so let your children disobey you. If you send them on an errand, let them never return to bring you word again.'

After shooting three arrows in three different directions Awole is said to have continued his curse, saying:

'To all the points I shot my arrows will you be carried as slaves. My curse will carry you to the seas; slaves will rule over you.'

Then dramatically Awole smashed an earthenware pot to the ground, saying:

'Broken calabash can be mended but not broken pot: so let my words be irrevocable.'

We cannot be too sure if Awole did utter all the words attributed to him. It is interesting, however, to note that for many years Oyo suffered the dreadful plight Awole had prophesied. Shortly after the revolt by Afonja followed by the Fulani take-over in Ilorin and the Fulani attack on Oyo, a series of civil wars broke out in the Oyo empire leading to general confusion and disaster.

Civil war

Afonja's successful revolt in Ilorin was a signal for a number of provincial rulers to seek to increase their own power at the expense of the central authority of Oyo. Life became insecure throughout Yorubaland as one Yoruba section fought against another and Yoruba enslaved Yoruba for export. The causes and the general course of the several wars that filled Yorubaland after the second decade of the nineteenth century are so complex that we may spare ourselves the trouble of sifting the details. A bare summary only may be attempted.

The Owu War was the first serious one of the civil wars. After the Owu had attacked some Ife towns, the Oni or ruler of Ife sent his forces against the Owu but they were surprised and defeated. Then the Ijebu joined forces with Ife in a fresh attack which resulted in a long siege and the final destruction of the town of Owu in 1825. The Owu subsequently fled into Egba country where they repeatedly fell foul of Egba local communities, taking captives for the slave markets on the coast. Carnage and enslavement became rampant throughout Yorubaland. In the wake of this unfortunate development large groups of people fled from their homes to seek shelter and safety in fresh abodes. Ibadan was founded in this process about 1829 when a mixed group of Ijebu, Ife and Oyo refugees settled on the site. In like manner Egba refugees founded Abeokuta about 1830.

As we have already seen, Dahomey took advantage of the difficulties of Oyo to free itself from Oyo domination. Attempts by Dahomey, however, to expand at the expense of Yoruba did not achieve any significant success.

Like the Dahomeans, the Fulani of Ilorin also sought to exploit Oyo's weak and confused condition to expand further south. Old Oyo was a constant target of Abdussalam's forces during the 1830s. After refusing to accept the Islamic faith, Alafin Oluewu made a last effort to throw out the Fulani from his capital. However this only evoked a fresh and more determined onslaught on Old Oyo by the Fulani. The capital was finally sacked and destroyed in 1837. The Fulani success was largely due to the fact that the Yoruba were unable to make common cause against the Fulani. Some Yoruba groups were even prepared to ally themselves with the Fulani against other Yoruba groups if it temporarily suited them.

Oluewu, who died in about 1835, was succeeded as Alafin by Atiba, said to be the son of Abiodun. Atiba made determined efforts to save and restore what was left of the heritage of the great days of Oyo. Atiba it was who chose the site for modern Oyo as the new capital for the kingdom. He both persuaded and coerced Oyo refugees and inhabitants of nearby villages to re-assemble in the new capital. However, it was Ibadan, some thirty miles to the south, that caught the imagination of the Oyo.

Ibadan and Abeokuta: new centres of influence

The importance of Ibadan and Abeokuta, both founded out of the confusion of the first half of the nineteenth century, lies in the efforts they made to restore stability in Yorubaland on a new basis. Both towns may be said to have struggled hard to meet the challenges posed by the difficult events of the time. So much has been said about the decline and decadence of Yoruba government and society during the nineteenth century that the real achievement of Ibadan and Abeokuta has sometimes tended to be over-looked.

From the time of its foundation Ibadan grew rapidly from strength to strength and soon became the most influential town in Yorubaland. In 1840 its soldiers turned back the tide of Fulani advance southward when they defeated a strong Fulani force from Ilorin at Oshogbo. However, unfortunately Ibadan was not always able to keep at peace with its neighbours. Its leaders intrigued against the authority of the Alafin based at New Oyo. Ibadan quarrelled and fought against the other influential Oyo centre of Ijaye to the north until that town was eventually destroyed by Ibadan forces. Ibadan was itself gripped by serious internal disputes. In spite of all this, however, Ibadan was able to establish a firm government largely based on a military aristocracy and was soon in control of a large number of towns spread over a vast area of Yorubaland. This area which constituted to all intents and purposes an Ibadan empire was ruled effectively.

The economy of Ibadan was largely based upon the extensive cultivation of farms around the town by the use of domestic slaves – captives from the various wars and campaigns conducted by Ibadan forces. With the wealth obtained in this way Ibadan was able to purchase firearms and ammunition from the coast and thus steadily achieved almost complete military ascendancy in Yorubaland. This was a significant revival of the glory that was Old Oyo's.

Abeokuta, founded about the same time as Ibadan, became the capital of the new Egba kingdom after the Owu war. Like Ibadan it grew rapidly and attained a position of influence in Yorubaland. However, the government of Abeokuta, unlike that of Ibadan, did not develop along the lines of a military aristocracy. It tried to achieve a kind of constitutional government based upon European-style democratic practices, largely due to the influence of Yorubas from Sierra Leone returning to settle in Abeokuta.

A significant feature of Abeokuta was its readiness in accepting European missionaries who were offered free lands to build churches and allowed to make converts. The missionary endeavour was greatly helped by the arrival in Abeokuta in the 1830s and 1840s of increasing numbers of Creoles of Yoruba origin (Aku, as they were called). Because of this development the British at Lagos showed keen interest in Abeokuta. When the Dahomeans attacked the town in 1851 they were eventually expelled through military aid given to Abeokuta by the British and the Church Missionary Society in Lagos. Thus Abeokuta during the second half of the nineteenth century became a kind of European post and a bastion of European civilization and influence in Yorubaland. This was of importance for the future expansion of European influence in that part of Nigeria.

Benin

Benin was one of the most remarkable of the old kingdoms of Western Africa. It started to flourish probably about the same time as the Yoruba kingdom of Oyo but boasts of an earlier dynasty older than that of Oyo. The modern dynasties of both Benin and Oyo claim descent from the legendary Oranmiyan, the prince of Ife, whose period is believed to date back to the early fifteenth or later fourteenth century. Benin City, capital of the kingdom of Benin, when first visited by Europeans in 1485 was described as a well-ordered and impressive city. It had broad and straight principal streets and its houses were arranged neatly in rows. The reigning king was in firm control of his realm. The Bini (as the citizens of Benin City are called) belong to a larger group of peoples known as the Edo. The Benin kingdoms proper extended some ninety miles from east to west and about thirty to forty miles from north to south. Benin City was situated almost in the centre of this area. The empire of Benin, however, extended on the north-east to the country of the Ishan and the Northern Edo, an area almost as large as the Benin kingdom proper. To the south-east Benin controlled the Urhobo and Isoko peoples. During its heyday the empire also covered the Ibo, living west of the Niger, and the Ekiti of Yoruba origin on the far north-west. Except the Ekiti and the Ibo, nearly all the other peoples of the empire were generally Edo-speaking; so that the kingdom and empire of Benin had the advantage of common linguistic and consequently cultural ties.

The king of Benin was known by the title Oba. Like the Alafin of Oyo the Oba was treated with exaggerated respect by his subjects. And again like the Alafin the Oba relied on certain classes of nobles and state officials to rule his subjects and administer his territories. The most notable of such state officials in Benin were the class of the old nobility called the Uzama who constituted a body of king-makers. The Uzama were responsible also for performing palace rituals including those connected with the installation of a new Oba. There is, however, one important respect in which the Oba's position was different from that of the Alafin of Oyo. Neither the Uzama nor any other chiefly class in Benin possessed anything like the dominating and restrictive powers that the Oyo Mesi held over the Alafin. No Benin state official or group of officials could compel the Oba to commit suicide as the Basorum could compel the Alafin to do in Oyo. It will be seen, therefore, that the Oba of Benin was constitutionally in a stronger position than the Alafin of Oyo. Furthermore, the fact that the Oba was succeeded by his eldest son gave considerable stability to the monarchy in Benin. In general the central authority was more stable in Benin than it was in Oyo. However to say all this is not to give the impression that the Oba had no checks on his powers: he was far from being an absolute ruler or a dictator. The Uzama and other palace chiefs had considerable influence on how the Oba ruled.

How then was the kingdom of Benin ruled? Besides Benin City, which was a large urban centre with a massive earth wall built around it, the rest of the kingdom consisted largely of a collection of small towns and villages. Each town or village or group of villages was under a chief known by the title Onogie*. Every Onogie assumed his chiefly position with the consent of the Oba to whom he was ultimately accountable. Twice each year the Onogie had to send to the Oba tribute collected locally in the form of yams and other foodstuffs. The Onogie kept for himself a proportion up to a half of the tribute he collected. In times of war each Onogie had to levy recruits for service in the Oba's army. The Onogie ruled his chiefdom with the assistance of a council of elders. Within the kingdom of Benin proper no Onogie nor council of elders could put a person to death, for all cases involving the death penalty were to be referred to the Oba's court in Benin City. There was thus a considerable check on the activities of the Onogie from the Oba's court, but in general the farther away a chiefdom was from the capital, the greater the freedom of action enjoyed by the Onogie.

* The plural is Enigie.

Careful organization and control of trade was an important feature in both kingdom and empire of Benin. Trade with Europeans from the coast always played an essential part in the economy of Benin. Inland markets throughout the empire were fed with European goods brought in from the coast by Benin traders as well as Itsekiri middlemen. Goods such as cloth, guns, powder and salt were sold in most parts of the empire. These goods were paid for with palm oil, ivory, kernels and, in early times, slaves. Long-distance trade was popular and particularly well organized for it offered very lucrative business. It was undertaken and almost monopolized by associations approved by the Oba. The Oba himself and some of the titled nobles of the Benin state took part in the long-distance trade on their own account. Well defined trade routes linked Benin City with Ilorin, Nupe and even Hausaland to the far north. The Oba derived considerable revenue from levies and taxes placed on visiting ships as well as the goods they carried. There were frequent quarrels and clashes between the Oba's customs officials and the European and Itsekiri traders operating in Benin.

Changing fortunes and loss of independence

During the first half of the nineteenth century the kingdom of Benin was generally in a strong position. Government was orderly. The empire may be said to have reached its apogee during this period.

In about 1804 Obanosa became the Oba of Benin when he succeeded his father Akengbuda, whose reign had covered the entire second half of the eighteenth century. Obanosa's comparatively short reign of thirteen years witnessed a bloody civil war in Benin. The war was brought about by the Oba's two sons who fought to contest their father's throne. The ill-effects of the civil war were, however, somewhat made good during the long reign of the next Oba, Osemwende (1816–48). The empire appears to have reached its territorial peak under Osemwende. Unfortunately, however, after Osemwende's death a period of decline followed. The accession of Oba Adolo in 1848 was greeted by a second civil war when Ogbewenkon, the Oba's brother, revolted and made the province of Ishan, of which his mother was a native, the base for serious incursions into Benin territory. The outlying districts of the empire, where the central authority had never been too well established in any case, took advantage of the confusion created by the state of war and proclaimed their independence, or acted as if they were virtually independent of the central government. However, in the face of all these troubles Adolo was able to keep his throne until his death in 1888. In the closing years of his reign he even tried to reassert the authority of the central government and to encourage trade in the kingdom.

In 1888 Ovonramwen became the Oba of Benin. The main event of his reign was the abrupt end of the independence of Benin through British

Ife head, called Olokun   Benin head, called The Princess

conquest. Like other independent West African states during this particular period of time, Benin became the victim of European imperialist forces. The story of Benin's fate follows a familiar pattern. Ovenramwen was invited by the British Vice-Consul in the British Protectorate of the Oil Rivers, established shortly before the Oba ascended the throne, to accept British protection over the kingdom of Benin. The Oba refused the offer. However, the British authorities were determined to absorb the kingdom of Benin into their Protectorate and in particular to get the Oba to open his empire freely to British trade. The Bini, who had had both trade and social relations with Europeans for upwards of three hundred years, had good reason for wishing to keep the British at arm's length. However, the Bini were not destined to be left alone. British traders and agents in southern Nigeria began to enlarge upon stories of atrocities and human sacrifice that reached them from Benin City. Itsekiri middlemen, who had suffered or become displeased by the Benin policy of restricting the trading activities of foreigners in the kingdom and empire, also went out of their way to exaggerate stories of human sacrifice and other barbarous acts in general committed in Benin.

The result of all this was a deliberate plan by British officers in the Protectorate to overthrow the kingdom of Benin. In early January 1897 a British party on its way to Benin is said to have been prevented from seeing the Oba and later ambushed and attacked. This provided the excuse for an attack on Benin City by a British expeditionary force. In spite of serious internal difficulties Oba Ovonramwen was able to resist the British attack for a little while but before long Benin City was conquered by British arms. In the general confusion of the British invasion a large number of slaves appear to have been put to death. It may be noted that the British invasion coincided with the celebration of the Ague festival which added to the spate of human sacrifice in Benin City. The British made great capital out of the extent of human sacrifice that the fallen city presented. Members of the British expedition looted precious collections of works of art from the Oba's palace including the now world-famous Benin bronze heads. These works of art of astonishing mastery revealed to the world the true quality of Benin culture and civilization.

Benin was declared part of the British Protectorate in Southern Nigeria, and Oba Ovenramwen was exiled from Benin. Thus came to an end the independence of one of the most stable and most remarkable kingdoms of West Africa. The overthrow of the kingdom came at a time of grave internal difficulties. The province of Ishan had been in revolt for some time. At about the same time Ibadan, which had become the most powerful Yoruba state, began to make serious incursions into the north-eastern parts of the Benin empire and to expand its own empire at the expense of Benin. It is, however, doubtful whether Benin could have successfully resisted determined British domination even if the kingdom had not been a prey to both internal and external dangers.

Questions

1. What were the effects of the domination of Dahomey by Oyo?
2. Describe the economic difficulties of Dahomey and how she attempted to solve them.
3. How was Dahomey able to shake off the domination by Oyo?
4. Show how Dahomey lost her independence to the French.
5. Why did the kingdom and empire of Oyo decline after Alafin Abiodun?
6. Describe the emergence and the importance of Ibadan and Abeokuta.
7. How was the Benin Kingdom governed?
8. Write a summary of the main events in Benin during the last twenty years of the nineteenth century.

For further reading

Akinjogbin, J. A., Dahomey and its Neighbours, 1708–1818, Cambridge University Press, 1967.
Biobaku, S. O., The Egba and their Neighbours, 1842–72, Oxford University Press, 1957.
Johnson, S., The History of the Yorubas, Lagos, 1937.
Omer-Cooper, J. D., Ayandele, E. A., Gavin, R. J. and Afigbo, A. E., The Growth of African Civilisation: The Making of Modern Africa (pp. 172–80), Longman, 1968.
Crowder, M., The Story of Nigeria (pp. 96–107), Faber and Faber, 1962.
Forde, D. and Kaberry, P. M., West African Kingdoms in the Nineteenth Century (pp. 1–91), Oxford University Press, 1967.
Burns, A. C. M., History of Nigeria, Allen and Unwin, sixth edition, 1963.

8 Iboland and the States of the Niger delta

The Ibos

Society and government

The main homeland of the Ibo people is the hinterland of the Niger delta to the east of the great river. Across the Niger to the west live the Western Ibos, some of whom were for many years within the Benin empire. In the delta itself there are considerable numbers of Ibos who have lived and worked for centuries alongside the delta peoples. The Ibos constitute the most numerous single group of the peoples in Southern Nigeria east of the Niger.

The Ibos were not organized in kingdoms as were Oyo and Benin, nor did they live under any other form of centralized government. The village virtually constituted the only effective political, social and economic unit: it was an entity in itself. A group of villages might have a number of common interests: they might use a common market or work together to maintain main paths. But rarely would a large collection of villages submit to the rule of a single person as king. Each village had a council of elders who directed its general affairs, but the entire village would assemble on occasions to discuss and take decisions on some vital issues. The Ibos were extremely egalitarian and independent-minded. Their society did not recognize classes of nobility based upon birth. There were titles that carried honour and prestige but these were available for all who merited them by virtue of deeds of manly courage or success in business.

The local village community was made up of various age groups, each of which bore special responsibilities for the good of all. The village society had its social norms and a strict sense of what was lawful and just. Its members allowed their daily lives to be governed and guided by such norms and concepts. Above all the strong belief of the Ibos in the supreme deity they called Chukwu gave remarkable religious colour to the life and work of every Ibo. All this helped to create effective government at the village or local level which adequately met the day to day needs of the Ibo people. In spite of the fact that the Ibos had no centralized government and thus had no equivalent whatsoever of the Oba of Benin, the Alafin of Oyo or the Asantehene of Asante, Iboland was in a sense a recognizable unit. All Ibos spoke a common language or naturally intelligible variants of it. As we have already seen, they all had a common concept of the supreme deity, Chukwu, from whom flowed common ideas of social justice. Furthermore, the incidence of trade, both internal and long-distance, brought various sections of Ibos into frequent contact. One significant source of intercourse was the practice of exogamy among the Ibos, that is, the practice whereby men took wives not from their own but from other villages. In this way there developed an interesting ramification of personal relationships over a considerable area.

Arochuku or Long Juju
Before the abolition of the slave trade the bulk of slaves sold by middlemen at various centres in the Niger delta were Ibos from the hinterland. After the evil trade had gradually been abolished in the course of the century, Iboland still played an important role in the economy of the region. A considerable proportion of palm oil products, which replaced slaves as the main economic preoccupation, came from the Ibo hinterland. Ibos played an important role in commerce in the main centres of the Niger delta.

In the absence of centralized government perhaps the most widespread Ibo institution of the nineteenth century was the Aro oracle, the famous or infamous Long Juju at Arochuku.

The Aro, a sub-section of the Ibo people, set up an oracle or mouthpiece of Chukwu, the supreme deity. They skilfully worked upon the deep-seated religious sentiment and fear of Chukwu throughout Iboland and the delta. As attendants of the oracle the Aro were both feared and respected almost universally. They used this fact to promote their trading activities and their economic position in general. They operated almost like a modern syndicate. They organized Aro settlements in all important centres in Iboland and the delta, especially along the main trade routes. Arochuku itself was conveniently sited on the Cross River at the mouth of which Calabar was situated.

During the period of the slave trade the Aro lured and sold into slavery unwary persons who came to consult the oracle. More often than not the Aro themselves would create situations which necessitated consultation of the oracle. Suspects who were hurried to the oracle to have their innocence or guilt established would mysteriously disappear. The Aro also used the oracle as a means of blackmailing wealthy persons and dispossessing them of their wealth. Long Juju, no doubt, became the most dreaded institution in both Iboland and the Niger Delta.

Such was the dominating influence of the Aro that the British operating in the Oil Rivers were led into believing that there existed what was virtually an Aro empire. This assumed empire they sought to incorporate into the British Protectorate of the Oil Rivers set up in 1885. Eventually a British expedition was sent to attack the shrine of Long Juju in 1902. This attack was followed by the gradual absorption of sections of the Ibos under British protection.

The City-States of the Niger Delta

The Niger delta, where the river in numerous outlets empties itself into the Gulf of Guinea after hundreds of miles of its sluggish journey from the Western Sudan, presents such a network of waterways as perhaps no other area of Africa has. In this region live some of the most vivacious and enterprising peoples of western Africa. The delta is the home of the Urhobo, the Kalabari, the Itsekiri, the Ijaw and the Ibeno, to mention only the most prominent peoples. As we have already seen a large body of Ibos have also for many years made their homes in the delta.

The delta peoples came into contact with Europeans from the late fifteenth and early sixteenth centuries. For nearly three hundred years the

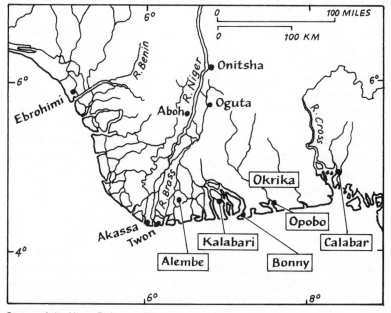

States of the Niger Delta, c. 1875

slave trade was the main pre-occupation of the peoples of the area. The wealth from this trade led to the emergence of settlements of a unique character in western Africa – the city-states. The interesting feature of these states was the variety of peoples each of them attracted. By and large, however, Warri had a predominant population of Urhobo and Itsekiri; Brass and Nembe of the Ijaw; Bakana of Kalabari; and Bonny of Ibeno. The city states were independent political units. Each was a busy commercial centre which boasted of a number of very wealthy self-made citizens. As among the Ibos, nobility by birth hardly existed among the delta peoples. A man obtained a position of prestige mainly through success in business. A slave could work his way to the very top as king of a city state.

The 'House' system

The most significant development of a socio-political nature in the city states of the Niger delta was the 'house' system. It was a complex system and all that we can do in such a brief survey is to outline its main features. Each city state was made up of a number of 'houses'. The 'house' was indeed a large business corporation or association consisting of both free men and slaves. At the head of each 'house' was a chief, a kind of director of the association. Under the chief were ranked sub-chiefs, free men and slaves. There was opportunity for the ambitious and enterprising member to advance to the very top. The heads of the various 'houses' in each city together constituted a kind of city council under the direction of a king, usually the most success-ful and influential head of a 'house'. Rivalry and competition between 'houses' were very common, if not the order of the day. Sometimes the situation could get out of hand and result in civil war.

For many years the main pre-occupation of the 'houses' was the slave trade. Each 'house' controlled a fleet of war canoes which brought in slaves or took trade goods into the hinterland. Wealthy 'houses' used some of their slave members to all intents and purposes as private armies. After the abolition of the slave trade in 1807, when the trade gradually declined until it was no longer profitable, the 'houses' quickly adjusted themselves to the situation and developed substitutes. The cultivation of large oil palm planta-tions with slave labour occupied the attention of most 'houses'. Some began to exploit the thick forests of the delta and the Ibo hinterland for timber.

Organization of trade

The life-blood of the states of the Niger delta was commerce. Trade was highly organized both during the period of the slave trade and that of legiti-mate trade. The principal commodity after the slave trade had been elimin-ated was palm oil. The richest palm oil producing areas were in the Ibo hinterland. The greatest oil markets were Brass, New Calabar, Bonny and

Opobo. A number of companies of European merchants, mostly from Liverpool in England, bought oil at the great markets. Middlemen of the delta kept the oil trade almost exclusively in their hands. The European merchants were not allowed to buy oil from the original producers: they had to buy it through the middlemen of the delta.

The usual practice was for the delta middlemen to obtain credits, sometimes huge ones, from the European merchants. The credits were in the form of goods such as cloths, guns, beads and copper rods. The middlemen would then take these goods into the interior for purchasing oil. Both the European merchants and the middlemen of the delta made huge profits for themselves at the expense of the ordinary oil producer and the consumer of trade goods. A good proportion of the goods the European merchants exchanged for oil were cheap and shoddy. The European merchants were usually a rascally lot and the oil trade in general was a very rough business in which all kinds of tricks were played. The European merchants were significantly called 'the palm oil ruffians'.

The African chiefs of the delta sought to control the oil trade as much as possible. They made their own regulations for the trade in their areas, and sometimes they combined to impose uniform regulations on the entire delta coast. A powerful chief would order a European merchant to appear before his court for a breach of the trade regulations. A European merchant who ignored the regulations could be banned from trade in a particular area. The most significant development in this respect occurred in Bonny, the most important centre for the oil trade, where a 'court of equity' was set up to deal with major cases between European and African traders. Leading members of the groups of European merchants, also known as supercargoes, took monthly turns to preside over this special court. The court laid down regulations which were binding, in theory, on both supercargoes and African middlemen. It used the boycott of offending parties as the principal weapon of enforcing its decisions.

By the mid-nineteenth century the Niger delta had become the most active commercial centre of British trade on the entire west coast of Africa. To promote conditions conducive to the development of British trade, consuls were appointed to the delta. These consuls, as we shall see later, played no small part in the gradual establishment of British authority not only in the Niger delta but also in Southern Nigeria as a whole.

Great leaders of the delta

King Pepple of Bonny

Bonny was one of the most active commercial centres of the Niger delta. Some of its heads of 'houses' became very wealthy – so wealthy that they were a threat to the king of the city. In 1835 one of the traders of the city, William Dappa Pepple, became King Pepple V of Bonny. There were a few 'houses' in Bonny that were richer and therefore more powerful than the king's own 'house', so there developed a struggle for power which ended in considerable loss of authority of the king. Pepple had other serious difficulties. His attempts to control trade by the European merchants in his kingdom led to hostility and intrigue on the part of the Europeans; and suddenly the king was plagued by ill-health.

It was during the period when King Pepple was being harrassed by troubles that John Beecroft was appointed English Consul in the Bights of Benin and Biafra. Beecroft was the most energetic English consul to have served in Southern Nigeria. He was determined to promote British trade at all costs and to establish British authority as much as he could. It was to such a man that the supercargoes in Bonny made endless complaints about illtreatment at the hands of King Pepple. Pepple in turn made counter-charges against the English traders in the area but Beecroft did not appear disposed to hear the king's story. The consul was at one with the English traders in believing that British trade could not thrive in Bonny, and indeed in the Niger delta as a whole until Pepple's power was crushed. Beecroft exploited the fact that Pepple's authority was under threat from his own overmighty subjects – a fact that led to a general state of unrest in Bonny. It is said that some English traders engineered an attack on some of their own fellow traders and blamed it on Pepple. In 1854 Beecroft intervened and, as current president of the court of equity, exiled Pepple from his kingdom altogether. A less able man than Pepple subsequently ascended the Bonny throne and further strife for power finally drove the state into a civil war. The chaos that ensued so badly affected trade that the European traders who had hailed Pepple's exile now canvassed for his return, believing that his popularity with the ordinary people would help to restore order. In 1861 Pepple was allowed to return to his kingdom and was paid a compensation of over £4,000.

King Jaja of Opobo

Jaja had been an Ibo slave who took service in a 'house' in Bonny. He was exceptionally gifted and was eventually to rise to the headship of his 'house'. He became a most dynamic figure in the delta and for years controlled its trade and politics. As head of the Anna Pepple House, Jaja found himself in opposition to King George of Bonny, the son and successor of King William Pepple. When civil war finally broke out in Bonny Jaja left the city with a large number of followers and in 1870 founded a new settlement which he later named Opobo. He became King Jaja of Opobo, and declared his new state independent of Bonny. Jaja was able to attract to his new kingdom fourteen out of the eighteen Houses of Bonny. Opobo soon became the most important state in the delta. The British consul and traders in the delta were both suspicious and afraid of Jaja and did their best to reduce his authority and influence. For Jaja had steadily increased his wealth and influence by virtually monopolizing the oil trade in the area if not on a greater part of the delta coast. His trading activities brought him into close contact with the Ibos of the hinterland and his name soon became a household word over a wide area.

Jaja's dominant position in the delta aroused what was to become the familiar reaction of the British in Southern Nigeria. The British consul, a man called Hewett, offered Jaja British 'protection'. But Jaja did not hide his hostility to the whole idea of British 'protection'. He sought clarification of the implications of 'protection' and assurances that it would not interfere with either his own authority or with the lands of Opobo. The consul appears to have reassured Jaja of his independence in somewhat vague terms. The crux of the whole matter was that the British traders were really unhappy about Jaja's influential position on the delta coast, especially as most other chiefs in the delta had by 1885 permitted themselves to be lured or coerced into accepting British protection. After trying persuasion without avail, the British finally decided on the use of force against Jaja. In 1887 they took advantage of trouble they themselves are suspected of having engineered in the kingdom of Opobo, and deposed Jaja, whom they exiled to the West Indies. The fall of Jaja was a significant victory for British supremacy in the Niger delta as a whole.

'The Blood Men' of Calabar

The story of the Blood Men presents a sad aspect of life in the Niger delta. It is a story of the oppression and eventual rebellion of a previously silent majority.

The general pattern of the 'house' system in the delta gave an opportunity to the lowly but ambitious and hardworking men to achieve distinction. The story of Jaja of Opobo, the slave boy who became head of a 'house' and subsequently king of a city-state, is a demonstration of this development. Among the Efik, however, the lot of the slave was a hard one. He was ill-used and even brutalized. He was, moreover, an easy victim for human sacrifice, especially on the death of his master. This situation eventually led to a bitter rebellion in Old Calabar. Calabar had been the centre of keen European missionary activity and the Christian teaching about the dignity of the individual and his freedom must have stirred numbers of slaves in and around the city. As a result of all this a political organization was started on a plantation on the Kwa River, the members of which styled themselves 'the Blood Men'. In 1851, when some members of this organization were arrested in Duke Town down the coast, spontaneous uprisings among the downtrodden slaves started at once. Plantations were destroyed by the slaves who also threatened the lives of their masters. It took some time and intervention by the European traders in the Calabar area who feared the consequences of the breakdown of order, to quell the rebellion.

The story of the Blood Men shows the misery and callousness that went side by side with the emergence of the wealthy class of middlemen in the Niger delta, at least among the Efik living to the east of the region. To such people as the Blood Men the gradual establishment of British authority in the delta must have been a welcome change.

Questions

1. Describe the main features of society and government among the Ibos.
2. Show the importance of Arochuku or Long Juju in Iboland.
3. How did the 'house' system work in the states of the Niger delta?
4. Describe the main pattern of trade in the Niger delta.
5. Explain the importance of the activities of King Pepple of Bonny and King Jaja of Opobo.
6. Who were 'the Blood Men' of Calabar? What does their career tell us about society in parts of the Niger delta?

For further reading

Dike, K. O., *Trade and Politics in the Niger Delta*, Oxford University Press, 1956.

9 The growth of British rule in Nigeria

Southern Nigeria

By the middle of the nineteenth century legitimate trade had developed considerably along the coast of what was later to become Nigeria, especially around Lagos in the west and in the Niger delta in the east. Gradually trade in slaves gave way to trade in palm oil which now became the principal commodity. Growing industrialization in various European countries led to an increased demand for palm oil, to the production of which several areas in Nigeria were particularly suited. After the middle of the century progressive exploration and opening up of the region bordering the Niger River in the north meant further expansion of trade. The commercial potential of the lands of Nigeria taken as a whole looked bright and reassuring. A large proportion of the trade was in the hands of British merchants whose interests became the concern of their home government; but Britain had other interests also. The suppression of the slave trade and its complete elimination remained a British commitment. There was also what may be called the missionary interest. During the course of the first half of the nineteenth century British Christian missions had been quietly but busily at work in various parts of Southern Nigeria: in Lagos and Abeokuta in the west; in Bonny and Calabar in the Niger delta; and in Onitsha deep in Iboland.

The general oversight of British interests was made the responsibility of appointed consuls. The first consulate was established in the Niger delta. When we come to consider that area in detail we shall hear more about the work of the consul. It need only be pointed out now that the consuls were generally devoted and able agents who played a significant part in the establishment of British influence and rule in Southern Nigeria.

The Crown Colony of Lagos
During the middle years of the nineteenth century Lagos received great attention from the British for two main reasons. In the first place the tenacity

shown by the rulers and people of Lagos in carrying on with the slave trade in spite of all efforts to persuade them to abandon it was a matter of great concern to the British. It appeared almost meaningless to try to discourage the slave trade elsewhere along the coast while it flourished openly in Lagos. Secondly, by the 1840s the growing importance of the palm oil trade in Yorubaland had greatly increased the value of Lagos as the main port to the vast hinterland. So for purposes of suppressing the slave trade and promoting the palm oil trade, a kind of control of local affairs in Lagos by the British was considered desirable. It was in such circumstances that John Beecroft was appointed British consul to the Bights of Benin and Biafra in 1849 with oversight of Lagos affairs. He was a most energetic official who saw as his single duty the advancement of British interests and influence. Beecroft's appointment may be said to mark a turning point in British relations with the states and peoples of Southern Nigeria.

For some time the kingship in Lagos had been the subject of dispute and strife. Two persons were particularly concerned with this situation. A younger man called Kosoko had succeeded in driving away from the throne an older contender called Akitoye. Beecroft, urged by the British merchants and missionaries in Lagos, supported Akitoye after securing a promise from him that he would help to stamp out the slave trade in Lagos. In 1851 Beecroft ordered a naval attack on Lagos. Although the attack was not very successful he was able to depose Kosoko and to instal Akitoye as king of Lagos. In a hastily concluded treaty with the British, Akitoye renounced the slave trade on behalf of his people and promised to do all he could to promote legitimate trade. Significantly too, Akitoye was made to agree to treat British merchants and nationals in his kingdom as most-favoured persons. A British vice-consul was appointed to Lagos to ensure that the terms of the treaty with Akitoye were observed.

However, Kosoko was not to be dismissed easily. He had a large following and enjoyed considerable influence even after he had been deposed. For the next ten years he threatened to attack Lagos and this prompted the British to keep a more vigilant eye on the town and to interfere more in the affairs of the kingdom than they might have normally done. When the old Akitoye died in 1853 the British consul to Lagos at the time, Campbell by name, managed to secure the election of Docemo, whom he thought he could control.

Meanwhile a difficult situation had arisen in the hinterland. Abeokuta, Ibadan and Oyo were once again involved in a fresh round of civil wars in Yorubaland. The unstable situation led to a sharp decline in trade passing through Lagos. The British, already worried about the poor prospects of trade, were jolted by the news that the French had secretly sent a delegation to Docemo. To forestall the French, the British consul and the British merchants in Lagos pressed the British Government to take steps to secure permanent control over Lagos. Subsequently in 1861 Docemo was prevailed upon to cede Lagos to the British for a pension of about £1,000 a year. The town and the area around it became a British Crown Colony. A governor was appointed for it and Britain obtained her first strong foothold in Nigeria. In spite of the often-repeated declaration that the British action in Lagos between 1851 and 1861 had been motivated by humanitarian considerations – namely to suppress the slave trade – the real factor was the need to secure British commercial interests.

The Yoruba hinterland
The cession of Lagos to the British had no effect on the turbulent situation in Yorubaland. If anything it created greater disquiet by arousing suspicion of British intentions. The civil strife continued unabated and the unstable situation it created began to engage the attention of the British at Lagos. It was strongly felt that the extension of British authority into the interior was necessary if order was to be restored. Governor Glover of Lagos thought that the best course open to him in promoting British interests was to inter-fere by force in the troubled situation in Yorubaland. In 1865 he dispatched a contingent of West Indian troops at his disposal in Lagos into the interior against the Egba who had attacked Ikorodu near Lagos, in an attempt to block the trade route to the coast. The defeat of the Egba by this British force was definitely an expansion of British authority beyond the confines of the Crown Colony of Lagos. The British Government disapproved of Glover's action.

The year 1865 should be remembered as a significant one in the period when Britain was groping for a policy towards West Africa. As we saw when discussing the affairs of the Gold Coast during this period, in that year a Select Committee was appointed by the British Government to review the British settlements in West Africa. The Committee not only recommended a limitation of British commitments: it even urged that the peoples in the British settlements in West Africa should be encouraged to assume con-trol of their own affairs as a prelude to an eventual British withdrawal alto-gether. All this was in line with current British thinking on colonies and British oversea trade in general. Colonies, it was felt, were expensive and not really necessary for the promotion of British commerce overseas. A few strategic points for the British Navy along the main trade routes of the world were all that was required. However, as had happened in the Gold Coast, it was soon to be realized in the case of Yorubaland also that the policy of aban-donment would not do. It would not secure the best interests of British trade in the end. The chaotic situation in Yorubaland demanded British interven-tion of some kind if conditions conducive to trade were to be achieved.

To Governor Glover the unrealistic quality of the recommendations of the 1865 Select Committee was clear. He believed that the root of the trouble in Yorubaland was the interruption of the trade with the coast by the Egba people. He attempted to mediate between the Egba and the Ibadan people but failed. The Colonial Office in London, to which he was responsible, would not approve of his use of force against any group of Yoruba. In the end Glover had to content himself with not altogether successful attempts to open the trade routes leading from the interior to Lagos. In 1871 he was able to summon a meeting of the rulers of a number of Yoruba states to talk peace, but nothing much came out of the effort. Soon afterwards he departed from Lagos as governor of the Colony. With Glover's departure from the Nigerian scene expansionism came to an end for the time being.

The civil wars in Yorubaland continued and appeared well-nigh interminable. They had gone on intermittently for nearly fifty years. All this adversely affected trade.

In 1886 the Governor of Lagos sent a delegation led by two ministers of religion including Samuel Johnson (a native of Oyo who later wrote an authoritative history of the Yoruba) to the warring Yoruba factions with a view to arranging peace. At long last the Yoruba leaders, except those of Ilorin, allowed themselves to be won over by the overtures for peace. Eventually representatives of the various factions, except Ilorin, met in Lagos to sign a general peace treaty. The independence of the various Yoruba states was confirmed. At this juncture the alarming report reached the Governor of Lagos that a French delegation from Dahomey had approached the Alafin of Oyo to negotiate for the conclusion of a treaty. The Governor hastened to forestall the French move by arranging his own treaty with the Alafin by which the Alafin agreed not to enter into a treaty with any other European power without the consent of the Governor. Shortly after this treaty the Egbado people in the south, harrassed by repeated attacks by their Egba neighbours, offered to place themselves under British protection. This was encouraging from the point of view of growing British influence.

When Sir Gilbert Carter arrived in Lagos as Governor he found that no true peace had yet been established in the interior. In 1892 Carter decided to send an expedition against the Ijebu of Awujale who had made themselves exceptionally difficult in all moves for peace. The expedition eventually took place and the Ijebu were defeated. This opened the door to a series of encroachments on Yorubaland by the British. The pacification of the Ijebu led to the free passage of trade to the delight of all those who stood to gain.

In 1893 Governor Carter embarked upon a great trek in Yorubaland. He was warmly welcomed in most places and he seized the opportunity to conclude treaties with the chiefs of the various Yoruba states. The Governor finally became an arbitrator in the inter-state disputes of Yorubaland and a British protectorate in all but name was established over Yorubaland. Thus at last many years of civil wars in Yorubaland were brought to an end through the diplomatic skill of Carter. The general atmosphere was now conducive to the development and expansion of trade. Roads were built to link up important centres in Yorubaland and a railway from Lagos to Ibadan was started.

The Oil Rivers Protectorate

British traders in the Niger delta were perhaps more involved in the affairs of the local peoples than elsewhere on the Nigerian coast. This was largely the result of the nature of trade and politics in the delta. The delta was the scene of cut-throat rivalry and competition in trade involving very close personal contact between the African middlemen on one hand and the European traders or supercargoes, as they were known, on the other. The delta, as we have already observed elsewhere, had a number of well-organized city-states dominated by energetic rulers and personalities who depended upon trade for their wealth and power. The delta was a unique area with its special problems of trade and politics. Because of all this it became necessary during the first half of the nineteenth century for British interests to be entrusted to consuls.

The volume of British trade in the delta mounted steadily. Palm oil, which was produced abundantly in the delta and its hinterland, was the principal article of trade. British supercargoes took their goods to the rivers at the Bights and exchanged them for palm oil. The progress of this trade depended on mutual trust between the supercargoes and the local inhabitants. It became necessary for the satisfactory conduct of trade to reach some sort of agreement between the two parties. Goods were sometimes taken on credit and arrangements had to be made for the collection of debts. Trade disputes had to be amicably settled. Supercargoes had to obtain right of entry into the rivers and creeks and of trade in particular areas. Such rights had to be guaranteed. Courts of Equity were set up in the rivers on which both supercargoes and local chiefs and their elders sat to see that trade regulations laid down were obeyed. However, with the best will in the world on the part of both supercargoes and local peoples, it required some form of overall supervisory authority or body to act as an umpire or arbiter between the supercargoes and the local traders, and over the various groups of European traders themselves. There was also the problem of supression of the slave trade. This many-sided supervision and oversight of British interests in the delta fell to the consul.

The first appointment as consul was John Beecroft, as we have already seen. He had lived on the West African coast for some twenty years before his appointment and possessed a wealth of experience in dealing with Africans. At first he had oversight of the entire coastline from Whydah to

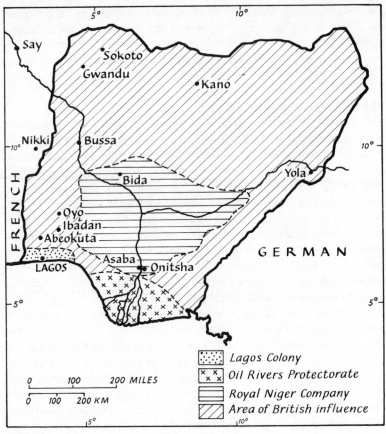

The areas of British influence, c. 1890

the Cameroons. In 1851, however, a vice-consul was appointed for Whydah, and in 1853 a separate consulate was established at Lagos, so that Beecroft was allowed more time for the supervision of the Niger and the Oil Rivers. The consul generally divided his time between the main British interests which had necessitated the setting up of the consulate at the Bights – protection of British commerce and suppression of the slave trade.

However, the consul possessed little real authority in dealing with disputes and difficulties that came before him in the rivers. His main source of power was the support of a British squadron of warships stationed in the area. The consul would generally make a show of force by sailing on the rivers in a man-of-war for which the local peoples seem to have had great fear and respect. But the support of the squadron was limited; a warship was not always available to take the consul round and, moreover, the fear of the warships was limited to the areas very close to the rivers. There were numerous creeks too small for the use of warships. However, when the consuls did have the support of the squadron they were able to use force with considerable effect against local chiefs who had defied their decisions or who had fallen foul of British traders.

Although the consuls acted with little real authority, in time the African chiefs and peoples of the delta, by and large, came to look on the consul as Governor of the Bights and brought their difficulties and disputes before him for settlement of their own free will. In this way the consulate began to be drawn more into the internal affairs of the states of the delta than the British Government was prepared to countenance.

The general reluctance of the British Government to sanction the expansion of British authority in West Africa has already been mentioned while discussing the situation in Yorubaland. This applied to the situation in the Niger delta also. However, the nature of trade and politics in the area necessitated British intervention of some sort.

By the 1880s, Britain had had openly to reverse her policy of non-intervention. One reason for this, as we shall discuss in some detail in another chapter, was the general state of rivalry and competition among the European powers for colonies in Africa: 'the scramble for Africa', as it has been called. This change affected British action in the Niger delta as in other parts, not only of Nigeria but also of West Africa in general. Having decided at last to establish her authority on the Nigerian coast, Britain instructed her consul in the delta to enter into a series of treaties with the chiefs of the entire area from Benin to the Cameroons. This policy finally led in 1885 to the proclamation of the British Protectorate of the Oil Rivers. Some of the more independent-minded rulers of the area resisted the proclamation. We have noted elsewhere how the able and ambitious King Jaja of Opobo resisted the absorption of his state into the Protectorate until he was overcome by a British force and was deposed and finally exiled to the West Indies in 1887. With Jaja out of the way the whole of the delta area soon fell within the Protectorate of the Oil Rivers.

In 1893 the Oil Rivers Protectorate became the Niger Coast Protectorate with the addition of a few more territories. We have already seen how, in 1897, the ancient kingdom of Benin was overcome by the British as the final step in the British control of Southern Nigeria.

It took some time and a number of expeditions before British authority could be established over Iboland in the hinterland of the Niger delta. The expedition leading to the destruction of the oracle of Long Juju in 1902 was part of the general pacification of Iboland. It was not till the second decade of the twentieth century that British administration was firmly established throughout Iboland.

The Niger Districts Protectorate

We have seen how the southern areas of Nigeria – the Crown Colony of Lagos, Yorubaland, the kingdom of Benin, the Niger delta and parts of Iboland – gradually came under British influence and eventual control during the second half of the nineteenth century. We now turn to the block of territory flanking the Niger and the Benue Rivers, an area stretching from Asaba northwards to Bida. It is a vast area roughly in the shape of an oval with Lokoja at the confluence of the Niger and the Benue almost exactly in the centre. British influence and control in this area followed the development of trade and we need to trace briefly this development to understand the political events that took place.

After a long search by a number of European explorers for the termination of the Niger, two brothers, Richard and John Lander, sailing from Bussa in the north eventually entered the sea at Brass Town in 1830. This successful discovery of the mouth of the Niger was greeted with speculations about the possibilities for trade that the river afforded into the interior. 'This long-sought-for highway into Central Africa was at last found. . . . To the merchant it offered a boundless field for enterprise; to the manufacturer, an extensive market for his goods, wrote an observer. However, this speculation proved rather extravagant: it took little note of the fact that the interior was almost entirely unknown and that the principal navigational difficulties from which the Landers had been spared were yet to be conquered. However, the discovery of the termination of the Niger and its possibilities as a waterway into the interior caught the imagination of merchants and within a few years expeditions began to explore possibilities for trade.

The first attempt to penetrate into the interior of the Niger with the view to opening up legitimate trade began in 1832—just two years after the discovery by the Landers—under Macgregor Laird, a Liverpool merchant. Richard Lander accompanied Laird and so did two other prominent persons, Dr Oldfield and Commander Allen who were sent by the British Government to survey the river. There was to be trade in palm oil on the river as the expedition moved up. This, it may be supposed, was to help towards defraying the cost of the expedition. Richard Lander, whose advice seems to have been much valued, was so enthusiastic about the potentialities for trade upstream that through his counsel it was decided to stake all on trade up the Niger. However, from the point of view of development of trade, the expedition was a failure. Opportunities for trade up the Niger fell far below expectations. The interior was unknown; the inhabitants of the delta were hostile to the development of trade upstream; and the outbreak of fever touched off the calamity. The expedition, however, increased knowledge of the interior and of navigation up the Niger and revealed pit-falls which could be taken into consideration in planning future expeditions.

After the failure of Laird's first expedition the next big attempt to develop trade on the Niger was made in 1841 when a large expedition was sent out by the British Government. This expedition was put under a Captain Trotter who had at his command three specially-built steamers. With Trotter were Commander W. Allen, Commander Bird Allen and Dr Thomson. The expedition was accompanied by missionaries, and materials were taken out for the establishment of a model farm. The mission was instructed to make treaties with local chiefs for the stoppage of the slave trade. It quite easily reached Lokoja on the confluence of the Niger and the Benue where a model farm was started. But soon sickness struck with a very high death-toll. Within two months forty-eight out of a total of a hundred and forty-five Europeans had died of fever. Bird Allen himself was dead and Trotter invalided. The people who had been left on the model farm at Lokoja were moved and the expedition was abandoned.

The failure of Laird's expedition of 1833 and of the 1841 mission created doubt and misgivings among humanitarians who had been filled with enthusiasm about the commercial potentialities opened by the Niger. An interval of a dozen years of no spectacular activity followed. The next active step to develop trade on the Niger was taken in 1852. The British Government agreed to furnish Laird with a suitable vessel for another expedition. As few white crew members as possible were to be taken. Naval officers were to be sent to survey the river; there were also to be a few people to look out for trade possibilities.

Beecroft, who had been chosen to command this third expedition having died before the expedition could reach West Africa, the command fell on Dr Baikie. With the use of quinine to prevent malaria not a single life was lost although Baikie's expedition spent sixteen weeks on the river. A good deal was learned about the Benue and about trade along the Niger, and for the first time a certain amount of legitimate trading was done upon the Niger. Of special significance, however, was the discovery that life could be made safe on the river by the use of quinine as a preventive. It was at last then proved that ships could remain in the river to trade: this was very important for the development of trade up the Niger. The first phase of the attempt to develop trade on the river – the pioneering and uncertain period – may be said to have been over.

Now the development of trade on the Niger could be pursued without great risk to health. It was clear, however, that trade could not yield appreciable profits for some time. A Government subsidy was therefore desirable to put trade on the Niger on a firm footing. In 1857 Macgregor Laird appeared on the scene again and entered into a contract with the British Government to send a ship each year to the Niger at the time of high water, the Government offering to grant him a yearly subsidy for five years on a diminishing scale. Hulks were established at Onitsha, Abo and Lokoja to serve as store-houses for the annual steamer. Educated Africans were largely employed. Salt, beads, cotton goods, spirits, guns and gunpowder were the articles in demand by the local peoples, for which they brought palm oil and some ivory in exchange.

After one of his ships had been attacked by local people (possibly delta men who were opposed to the development of trade upstream) Macgregor Laird appealed to the British Government for protection. Consequently, the squadron was ordered to make a warship available for the protection of Laird's steamer.

Baikie had stayed on in Lokoja for some time and was styled Consul. Laird died in 1861 and Baikie's own death followed in 1864, but the development of trade that had so far been achieved on the Niger was not allowed to perish. The directors of the Manchester Cotton-Growing Association, who saw prospects of cotton cultivation on the Niger, were in favour of a government subsidy and encouragement to the merchants trading up the Niger. However, the Liverpool merchants engaged in the palm oil trade in the delta were vehemently opposed to the development of trade with government help on the Niger. They did not like the idea of the inland traders tapping their own supplies of palm oil. From this point the Niger plan was thrown into some confusion. The delta merchants and their African middlemen attacked the steamers and trading posts of the inland traders and did everything they could to impede the progress of their rivals. The settlement at Lokoja was blockaded by hostile Africans for almost half a year and in 1869, owing to the difficulty of protecting the settlement, the Lokoja consulate was closed. Warships, however, paid occasional visits to protect trade in general. However, the effective protection of British trade in the area after the withdrawal of the consul from Lokoja was largely owed to King Masaba of Nupe. The king, who needed firearms to maintain his throne against the claim of rivals, showed keen interest in the promotion of trade in general with the Europeans.

It was becoming clear that unity of some sort among the merchants trading on the Niger was needed. The hard facts of the situation and the persuasion of one of the most far-sighted and influential men on the Nigerian scene during the second half of the nineteenth century, Sir George Goldie Taubman, brought the various inland trading companies to realize that unity alone could preserve their interests. In 1879 the various companies trading on the Niger were amalgamated under the name United Africa Company. Three years later its name was changed to National Africa Company.

In 1886 Goldie's Company changed its name once again when it received a charter and became known as the Royal Niger Company. The charter

empowered the Company to administer territories along the Niger whose
rulers were willing to enter into treaties for this purpose. In 1887 a British
Protectorate was formally proclaimed over all those lands whose chiefs had
signed treaties with the Company. The Royal Niger Company had a difficult
task trying to administer the vast territory it had acquired. It established its
headquarters at Asaba on the Niger. Contrary to the spirit of its charter the
Company established a monopoly over trade on the Niger. Other traders
and trading groups were restricted in the territories under the control of the
Company. The African traders of the Niger delta bitterly resented the
Company's discrimination against them. In 1895 the Brassmen were compelled to make a serious attack on the Company by raiding its port at Akassa.

The Royal Niger Company persistently and successfully kept the French
and Germans from intruding into the territory in which it operated and so
saved it for Britain at the time of the partition by European powers. This
situation was almost a personal triumph for Sir George Goldie.* He had not
received the support he wanted from the British Government in his attempts
to shut out the French in particular from the lands of the Niger. By 1884 he
had concluded no fewer than thirty treaties of friendship and understanding
with local African chiefs.

Northern Nigeria

The last extensive area of Nigeria to come under British rule was the North.
The Royal Niger Company was again largely responsible for winning the
huge savannah lands of Nigeria's north for Britain. France followed up her
conquest of Dahomey in 1892 by attempts to spread French influence
over the territories to the north-east of that country. The Fulani empire,
which covered nearly the whole area we are about to consider, was France's
ultimate target. However, this was the very area Sir George Goldie and the
Royal Niger Company were anxious to win for Britain.

Goldie foresaw the wider implications of France's acquisition of Dahomey
in the great scramble for territories in West Africa that was raging at the
time. He immediately tried to secure the old state of Borgu on the Niger for
his Company by entering into a treaty with the Sultan of Sokoto, said to be
the overlord of Borgu. The French, however, quickly pointed out that Sokoto
was not the overlord of Borgu but Nikki, a town now situated in the modern
Republic of Dahomey and just outside the Nigerian border with that country.
This controversy led to one of the most dramatic races for acquisition of
territory in the colonial history of West Africa. A French mission led by a
Frenchman called Decoeur, and a British team under Captain Lugard (later

* George Goldie Taubman had changed his name.

Sir Frederick Lugard) vied with each other to reach Nikki and obtain a treaty that would grant access to Borgu and control of it. The British won the race, having arrived in Nikki five days ahead of the French. Lugard, by a mixture of persuasion and bluffing, got the treaty he wanted from the King of Nikki. Having secured Borgu as a British sphere of influence, Goldie quickly moved into Nupe where he sent forces of the Royal Niger Company, ostensibly to suppress the slaving activities carried on by the Emir or ruler of Nupe. Goldie's next target was Ilorin, lying just south of Borgu. Thus within a short period of time, the Royal Niger Company had succeeded in stealing a march over its French rivals and subsequently obtained for itself a large block of territory on the Niger in the north. France hotly denounced the British action in Ilorin and Goldie decided to make a show of force by getting Lugard to take command of a battalion of the West African Frontier Force in readiness for action although Goldie did not actually want to fight the French. Nor were the French themselves interested in war with the British. Negotiations subsequently took place between the British and the French, ending in a line dividing the spheres of influence of the two powers. This arrangement left Ilorin and Borgu to the British but Nikki itself went to the French.

The Royal Niger Company had done extremely well in securing Northern Nigeria for Britain. However, the Company was faced with the difficult problem of administering the vast territory for which it was now responsible. Meanwhile the Company's monopoly of trade on the Niger as a whole had made it very unpopular and open to vehement criticism. In 1899 the British Government decided to revoke the charter of the Company. The Company was duly compensated for its loss and the Government bought up some of its assets in the form of buildings. The Company's territories were formally taken over by the British Government on 1st January 1900. The whole of Nigeria was re-organized under three main administrative areas. Lagos remained a Crown Colony with a fringe of protectorate around it. The various protectorates of the south were amalgamated into the Protectorate of Southern Nigeria. Lastly the northern areas were organized as the Protectorate of Northern Nigeria after its borders had been agreed upon with the French.

Lugard and Northern Nigeria
Lugard was appointed to try to put together and administer the areas now placed under British rule in the Protectorate of Northern Nigeria. No one appeared to have any clear idea of the extent of the territories or the variety of peoples involved. Some areas had yet to be pacified and some local rulers to be convinced about their loss of independence. It took military campaigns before Lugard could proclaim that the Fulani empire was no more and that Britain was the new master.

The first serious trouble came from the Emir of Kano who had openly defied British authority. Lugard sent an expedition against the old walled city which was forced to surrender in early 1903. The surrender of Kano virtually marked the formal collapse of the Fulani empire. Sokoto, which was next to resist British authority, quickly submitted. One notable fact was the attitude of the Hausa populace as distinct from the Fulani of the ruling classes. The Hausa subjects showed little or no concern about the resistance to the British. They went about their daily duties and accepted the change of masters without fuss.

Lugard tackled the difficult problem of administering the huge Protectorate seriously and realistically. In the absence of adequate administrative personnel and resources, he resorted to the so-called system of indirect rule which was by no means new to British administration. Indirect rule was essentially a common-sense approach to governing without the necessary personnel and resources. Lugard took over the fundamentals of Fulani government. The Emirs and other local rulers were allowed to continue to rule their people but under the general supervision of British officers stationed at the main centres and other vantage points. The spirit of British law and justice was applied.

Unification of Nigeria

For nearly one and a half decades the Protectorates of the South and the North were administered separately. However, there were sound reasons for unification of some sort and Lugard planned and worked towards this end. The South had far greater resources than the North. The North was really run at a deficit and for some time a subsidy from the British Government was necessary. Railways had to be built to link up the country as a whole and there was a need for overall economic planning. In 1914 the two Protectorates were amalgamated and Nigeria was unified. However, Lugard had planned that the North should maintain some of its distinct features and, so to speak, should be preserved from undue 'contamination' of the comparatively more progressive South. This policy had far-reaching consequences for the future history of Nigeria.

Questions

1. Why were the British very interested in the affairs of Lagos about the middle of the nineteenth century?
2. Why were the British in Lagos anxious that the wars in the Yoruba hinterland should cease?
3. Describe the attempts made by Governor Glover and Governor Carter to bring order to the Yoruba hinterland.
4. How did the British consuls spend their time in the Oil Rivers?
5. Describe the attempts made to establish trade on the Niger between 1830 and 1850.
6. What were the achievements of the Royal Niger Company? Why was the Company's charter withdrawn?
7. What part did Lugard play in winning Northern Nigeria for the British and in administering the area?

For further reading

Crowder, M., *The Story of Nigeria* (pp.155–90), Faber and Faber, 1962.

Jones, G. I., *The Trading States of the Oil Rivers*, Oxford University Press, 1963.

Lloyd, C., 'Dr. Baikie and the Niger', *History Today*, October 1971.

10 The partition of West Africa

Factors leading to the partition

We have already noted in previous chapters how some parts of West Africa came under European rule. We have seen British action in this respect in Sierra Leone, the Gold Coast and Nigeria, and French action in Dahomey. We have a few gaps to fill in now to complete the story of the European powers' scramble for colonies in West Africa. But first, what were the main factors underlying the scramble for colonies?

By about 1870 there was hardly any important area in West Africa not known to Europeans. Expeditions to the Niger had led to a considerable body of information about the lands and peoples in that part of West Africa. In the far west of West Africa the Senegal and Gambia Rivers offered ready means for penetrating deep into the interior. In the southern regions the activities of European missionaries and traders had led to valuable contacts with many of the inhabitants. However, in spite of all these developments, with very few exceptions, European authority was restricted to the coastal areas throughout West Africa. Except in Senegal in the case of the French; and in the Gambia, Sierra Leone, the Gold Coast and Lagos in that of the British, there was no significant official European involvement in the affairs of Africans. Generally speaking, Europeans had not really started to grapple with the problem of ruling Africans. Then suddenly within the short space of two decades (1880–1900) the whole of West Africa (except for Liberia) was partitioned into European colonies.

What were the causes of this change? In the first place, a great change had occurred in the attitude of European powers towards Africa. Before the last quarter or so of the nineteenth century Great Britain had led the way in the mass production or manufacturing of goods by machines in factories. This great change has been called the Industrial Revolution. For many years British goods met with little or no competition in markets throughout the world. The raw materials of all parts of the world had been at Britain's disposal. This unique position led Britain to advocate and champion free trade.

But then after about 1870 the position changed. Other European countries, in particular France and Germany, began to industrialize rapidly and to challenge Britain's hitherto privileged position. The industrial and commercial competition and rivalry which followed led to the feeling that, if each of the great industrial powers could monopolize the markets and raw materials in specific areas of Africa and Asia, then it would be ensuring its advantage in the fast competing world. In other words the acquisition of areas of influence and of colonies was considered very conducive to the promotion of European commerce and industry. West Africa was wholly caught up in this idea and development.

Secondly, an important development in the vast area of Central Africa now known as the Republic of the Congo, hastened the process of colonization elsewhere in Africa. King Leopold II of the Belgians had created a personal empire for himself in this area of Africa. King Leopold's monopoly of a vast rich area conflicted with the wishes and ideas of Britain and other leading European nations, notably France and Germany. To resolve the controversy over the situation an international Conference was arranged in Berlin in 1884. It was declared by the Berlin Conference that all nations should have free access to the interior of Africa. A more important further declaration was the one that no European annexations or protectorates in Africa would be taken as valid unless there was clear evidence of effective occupation. The rivalries of the European powers, whetted by the Conference, developed into a scramble for colonies, led mainly by Germany in the years following 1885. This accounts for the race for treaties with African

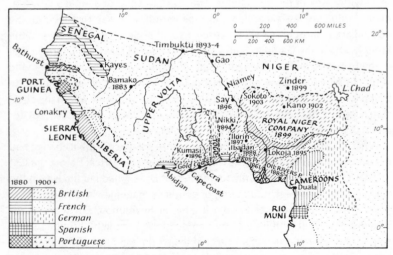

European advance in West Africa

rulers between officials of the Royal Niger Company and French agents in Northern Nigeria and the adjacent areas. It also explains why the French and the British took steps to conquer Dahomey and Benin respectively, to cite only these examples.

Thirdly, there is what may be termed the psychological aspect of the scramble for colonies. A kind of national prestige came to be associated with the possession of colonies although in reality some colonies were by no means assets to the colonizing powers. Britain was seen by others to be a great country, and this greatness was connected with her possession of colonies. So Germany too had to have colonies (to appear great!).

Fourthly, European missionaries and traders operating in various parts of West Africa normally wished to be left alone to pursue independent action. However, when threatened in one way or another, they would petition their home governments to protect them and safeguard their interests by annexing the areas in which they were operating.

Lastly, there was one important development outside Africa which had a remarkable effect on the process of colonization in Africa including West Africa. In 1870 Otto von Bismarck, Chancellor or Prime Minister of Prussia, the most important of the German states, humiliated France by inflicting a crushing victory on her. Germany became a united country after this victory. A rich district of France called Alsace-Lorraine was annexed by Bismark's Germany as part of the final peace settlement between the two countries. Thereafter, Bismarck took great pains to do two things: to prevent France from brooding so much over her loss of Alsace-Lorraine as to think of revenge; and to avoid an alliance between France and Britain in particular against Germany. Bismarck cultivated these aims with great zeal and care. He deliberately encouraged France to seek colonies in Africa, hoping that, while compensating herself for her loss of territory in Europe, France might clash with Britain in a struggle for colonies and would thus not enter into an alliance with Britain. The plan appeared to have worked out superbly when France entered the colonial race in Africa against Britain in full force. For some time Bismarck himself tried to avoid his own country involving itself in the colonial struggle, but groups of Germans became so enthusiastic and enchanted about acquisition of territories that he was at last compelled to let his countrymen satisfy themselves. So during the last two decades of the nineteenth century we see in West Africa a scene resembling a pack of hunting dogs let loose in a game reserve. It was in this general welter of ideas and factors that the explosive scramble for colonies in West Africa took place between 1880 and 1900. This was, in fact, sparked off in 1879 by the French advance from Upper Senegal in the direction of the Niger.

Before we turn to other aspects of the partition we need to caution ourselves by one or two observations. It has been suggested by some writers on the partitition that one of the main reasons why European powers came seeking for colonies in Africa was so that they might send out their surplus and unwanted population. This cannot apply meaningfully to West Africa for practically nowhere in that part of the African continent has the white man succeeded in making his permanent home. It used to be called the 'White Man's Grave'. Although medical science and knowledge did a great deal to reduce the danger, by the end of the nineteenth century Europeans were still doubtful about settling permanently in West Africa. Even in eastern Africa, where climatic conditions can be favourable to Europeans, they were, by and large, slow in making their permanent homes there during the period of the scramble. It may be noted that it was with some reluctance that the British Government accepted responsibility for Uganda – even at the very end of the nineteenth century. In 1894 the English magazine called *Punch* carried a cartoon of John Bull, a powerfully built man, representing Britain, opening his door in the morning and finding a black baby labelled Uganda abandoned. John Bull exclaimed 'what, another . . . well, I suppose I must take it in'. The so-called White Highlands of Kenya did not become popular with Europeans until well into the twentieth century – after the First World War. So we have to be cautious in linking the partition of West Africa by European powers with the problem of over-population in European countries.

French and German acquisitions

If Britain had shown interest in the acquisition of colonies in West Africa in the first half of the nineteenth century it would have acquired a good deal more than it did at the end of the period of the scramble. We have seen how in 1865 the report of a Select Committee typified British reluctance to accept the inconvenience of ruling Africans. British gains in the scramble consisted largely of the acquisition of territories around its existing settlements of Sierra Leone, the Gold Coast and Lagos in Nigeria. France made the most impressive gains in West Africa in so far as size is concerned. French forces, largely made up of Senegalese troops, swept through the Western Sudan from the Senegal to the Chad, in a remarkable advance. The open nature of the country was of advantage to the French in this advance.

During the fifteen years or so after 1850 France had built up her position firmly in the Senegal, thanks to the energetic policies of Faideherbe, French governor in the area during this period. When the colonial scramble began in the 1880s French forces based on Senegal pushed steadily eastward. We have already told the full story in an earlier chapter of the clash between French forces and Samori Toure from 1882. Samori was taken prisoner by French troops in September, 1898, and was exiled to the Gabon where he died two years later. In their general sweep through the Western Sudan French forces occupied Bamako, capital of the modern Mali Republic, on the upper Niger. In 1894 they occupied Timbuktu also, and within a few years France was in control of the vast area that became known as the French Sudan. After signing numerous treaties with local chiefs, France proclaimed protectorates over the lands of the Mossi of the Upper Volta.

On the Guinea Coast we have already discussed how France conquered the proud kingdom of Dahomey in 1892 and brought the Porto Novo and Anecho areas under her protection. French interests had existed in the Ivory Coast for many years. In 1886 the French Government took over control of the area from French merchants operating there. The negotiation of treaties finally ended in the fixing of the present boundaries of the Ivory Coast. A brief look at a map of West Africa before the period of independence (p. 132) will give an idea of the enormous area that France had acquired by the end of the nineteenth century.

There had been German interests in West Africa earlier in the century. By 1884 there were a number of German firms trading in various parts of West Africa and in other parts of the African continent. German missionaries had been active in parts of West Africa for many years. For example German missionaries had been doing valuable work in education and in preaching the gospel in the Gold Coast as far back as 1828. In 1884, on the eve of the Berlin Conference, what may be described as official German colonial policy emerged: the German flag should follow and protect German traders in such territories as they operated.

Germany acquired two colonies in West Africa: Togo and the Cameroons. She literally snatched both before Britain and France were aware of it. There had been German missionaries in both territories, but in the Cameroons German interests were relatively small. In July 1884 a special Commissioner was sent out to West Africa by the German Government in the person of Dr Nachtigal. His mission was ostensibly to inspect German interests in West Africa. He secured treaties from African chiefs both in Togo and the Cameroons. Britain became suspicious of Dr Nachtigal's real mission and instructed the British Consul in the Bights of Benin and Biafra to obtain treaties of friendship from local chiefs. The consul found himself five days too late.

From their footholds on the coast the Germans pushed progressively inland. German penetration of the Cameroons met with considerable resistance and did not reach the Lake Chad region until 1902. However, in general, Togo was peacefully acquired and proved by far the more successful of the two German West African colonies. Its economy was fairly buoyant and its people well accustomed to internal trade.

Questions

1. What were the principal factors that led to the partition of West Africa?
2. Account for the enormous gains made by the French.
3. How did the Germans acquire Togo and the Cameroons?

For further reading

Fage, J. D., *A History of West Africa* (pp. 160–74), Cambridge University Press, 1969.

11 West Africa under colonial rule

The main colonial powers that emerged in West Africa after the scramble for colonies were France, Britain and Germany. As far as size was concerned France, as we have seen, made the most impressive gains. The French possessions had the advantage of continuous territory. It was thus possible for France to treat her colonies as a single large unit. In Nigeria Britain acquired a colony larger in size and perhaps with a greater variety of peoples than her three other West African colonies of the Gambia, Sierra Leone and the Gold Coast. In terms of population Nigeria was certainly larger than all the rest of West Africa, French and British. Germany finished third with Togo and the Cameroons.

Because of limitations of personnel and resources the system of indirect rule was applied in varying degrees by both France and Britain. Each of the colonial powers had its own colonial philosophy and peculiar ways of dealing with its colonies.

British colonial policy and rule

In all the territories that became her West African colonies, Britain had had old settlements before the period of the scramble. As already pointed out, in Nigeria she made enormous additions, and in Sierra Leone and the Gold Coast quite considerable gains. Britain had acquired reasonable knowledge and experience of dealing with African peoples in her former settlements. However, the problems of administration that faced her after the end of the colonial race, especially in the case of vast Nigeria, were great and very challenging indeed. In attempts to grapple with the difficult situation Britain tried out the system of indirect rule in West Africa. Northern Nigeria was the main area for the experiment. Faced with the problem of administering the vast territories and varied peoples of Northern Nigeria with neither the necessary personnel nor resources, Sir Frederick Lugard, as governor, was compelled to make use of the existing system of administration in the conquered Fulani emirates. For after all the Fulani system had proved effective for almost a century. Ruling indirectly through the existing system was a commonsense solution for the problem Lugard had on his hands. As a matter of fact indirect rule was not a new creation: it had been resorted to by the British in India.

What was indirect rule, and how did it operate in Northern Nigeria? Lugard himself described it in the following words: 'The system of Native Administration in the separate Government of Northern Nigeria had been based on the authority of Native Chiefs. The policy of the Government was that these chiefs should govern their people, not as independent but as dependent rulers. The orders of Government are not conveyed to the people through them, but emanate from them in accordance, where necessary, with instructions received through the Resident. While they themselves are controlled by Government in matters of policy and of importance, their people are controlled in accordance with that policy by themselves. A political officer would consider it as irregular to issue direct orders to an individual native, or even to a village head, as a General commanding a division would to a private soldier, except through his commanding officers. The courts administer native law, and are presided over by native judges. Their punishments do not conform to the criminal code, but, on the other hand, native law must not be in opposition to the ordinance, of Government, which are operative everywhere, and the courts are under the close supervision of the District Staff. Their rules of evidence and their procedure are not based on British standards, but their sentences, if manifestly faulty, are subject to revision. Their prisoners are confined in their own gaols, which are under the supervision of the British staff. The taxes are raised in the name of the native ruler and by his agents, but he surrenders the fixed proportion to Government, and the expenditure of the portion assigned to the Native Administration, from which fixed salaries to all native officials are paid, is subject to the advice of the Resident, and the ultimate control of the Governor. The attitude of the Resident is that of a watchful adviser rather than of an interfering ruler, but is as jealous of the peasantry and the injustice to them'.

In brief, Lugard was governor for the whole of Northern Nigeria. The larger sub-divisions or provinces were under the charge of Residents who were directly responsible to the governor. Each province had further sub-divisions or districts, each under a district officer responsible immediately to the Resident. It was through this hierarchy or pyramid of British officials, from the governor down to the district officer, that Northern Nigeria was administered in the manner described by Lugard.

Indirect rule as applied in Northern Nigeria suited the situation in the former Fulani emirates. It should, however, be noted that the Fulani emirates were not co-extensive with Northern Nigeria; they did not cover the entire

North. In the 'middle belt' as a whole, were numerous peoples like the Tiv and Idoma, with whom the political situation was more like that in Ibo country. In other parts of British West Africa indirect rule had to be modified to suit local conditions. The system worked quite well in some places; in others it showed serious defects. In areas where centralized administration had not existed before, where local government had always remained at the level of the village or cluster of villages, the Lugard plan was not very successful to begin with. For example, among the Ibos, where centralized government was absent, it became necessary to create larger units to make the indirect rule principle meaningful. In the process chiefs were created where none had existed before. The authority of such chiefs was without a natural basis and suspicion and lack of confidence resulted. Even in some of the highly centralized administrative areas such as the emirates in Northern Nigeria, the Yoruba states, and among the Asante in the Gold Coast, the whole business of indirect rule was often seen by the local peoples as curtailing the authority of the local chiefs and rulers. This led to trouble; for it removed the effective co-operation that was the prerequisite for smooth government by a handful of British officers. Inexperienced British officers tended to interfere unnecessarily in matters they did not fully understand and rushed in where angels would fear to tread. Vital customs and practices were violated and taboos broken with bitter results. This did happen in Asante, where it became necessary for the British Government to send Captain Rattray, an anthropologist, to study and offer advice on local customs. We could go on citing examples of this kind of drawback but the main point is that indirect rule did not always work smoothly. It sometimes worked against itself by undermining the local authority it set out to direct and harness. However, the system in various forms remained the basis of British colonial rule and on the whole did achieve some success.

What were the goals of British colonial policy? In the early years of the colonial era a number of British colonial officials in numerous letters and articles attempted to justify British rule in Africa and to explain the ultimate purpose of this rule. Lugard led the way in this exposition by his *Dual Mandate*. Britain, according to Lugard, would benefit from the development of the vast resources of Africa but at the same time she owed an obligation to bring greater benefits to the African peoples too. The exploitation of the resources of Africa should improve the living standards of the Africans. Some British officials became worried about the disruption of African culture by the impact of Western ideas. As a result of this a frantic attempt was made to protect the less advanced societies such as existed in the northern parts of Nigeria and the Gold Coast. Efforts in this direction led to an attempt to protect such societies from 'contamination' by the more enlightened elements of the coastal regions. This policy of partial isolation can hardly be said to have achieved the desired aims. For, as it turned out, through such policy some sections of the colonial territories lagged behind their coastal neighbours in the march towards modernization.

In the southern and coastal areas of the four British West African colonies progressive educational facilities and gradual acquisition of considerable wealth by Africans made it desirable to involve some colonial subjects in the process of administration. In the earlier period the colonial governors were assisted by small bodies of British officials who constituted executive councils. At the same time legislative councils were established. The majority of the members of the legislative councils were British officials. However, gradually increasing numbers of African unofficial members were admitted. Although the legislative councils were used in passing laws, they could not initiate any laws nor had they real power over the way the governors administered the colonies. By the end of the colonial period Sierra Leone, the Gold Coast and Nigeria had legislative councils with unofficial majorities, but the governors possessed powers of veto which empowered them to set aside decisions of the legislative councils in the interest of the public good.

In the principal towns like Bathurst, Freetown, Accra and Lagos, municipal and town councils were set up. These councils had elected representatives and gave valuable services in local administration and the provision of amenities. The inference from all this is that British colonial policy had in view the gradual training of Africans to take over eventually the management of their own affairs in the various colonies. This policy was often declared by senior British officials; but the growing African elite found the pace and process painfully slow and so began to press for fuller participation in government for themselves. If eventual self-government and independence for the colonies was the ultimate goal of British colonial rule in West Africa, this goal was seen by the British themselves to be in the distant future. In the mid-1940s a single university institution was planned to serve both Nigeria and the Gold Coast. The pace at which the colonial peoples in both colonies wanted self-government may be said to have been woefully underestimated, for within a few years of this plan independence was in the air and a single university for both countries was considered not only inadequate but also incompatible with national prestige and aspirations.

French colonial policy and rule'

Although the French had been active in parts of West Africa for many years before the period of the scramble for colonies, they had not acquired the same experience in dealing with Africans as the British had. French experience had been limited to small urban communities in Goree, Dakar and St Louis. When France conquered the Senegal between 1854 and 1865 it adopted a unique approach for dealing with the Africans of the colony. As we have seen in an earlier chapter, a few Africans were regarded as French citizens and they had the same rights and privileges as Frenchmen in Paris. Some such French Africans could even sit in the French National Assembly in Paris. But the rest of the Africans in the colony were French subjects and not French citizens. The expectation, however, was that as these African French subjects acquired education and the French way of life they could eventually become French citizens. So it may be said that the ultimate policy was that the Africans in the Senegal could progress gradually to becoming French citizens with full rights of Frenchmen.

During the last two decades of the nineteenth century, when France rapidly acquired the enormous territory of French West Africa, the problem of dealing with the variety of peoples in the new French colonies was enormous. The policy that had been applied to the Senegal was not found suitable for the new areas. France subsequently adopted a kind of indirect rule that was more rigid and narrower in scope than the British system. The policy of assimilation, that of gradually turning Africans into French citizens, did not work fast enough in French West Africa. Most Africans in the French colonies remained at the level of French subjects. Village chiefs or headmen were recognized or created for the purpose of administration. These chiefs or headmen acted as agents for French administrators; but their powers were very much limited.

French colonial rule rested on a pyramid of French officials. The whole of French West Africa eventually came to be regarded as one administrative unit. At the head of this administration was a governor-general resident in Dakar in Senegal. Each colony – the Ivory Coast, Sudan, Upper Volta, Niger, Mauritania and Dahomey – had a governor responsible to the governor-general in Dakar. Under each governor was a hierarchy of French officials down to the district officer. The governor-general was responsible to the National Assembly in Paris through a member of the French Government.

The policy of assimilation broke down because of the difficulties in the way of the Africans who aspired or were made to aspire to it. In fact, by about 1900, French ideas of assimilation had given way to 'association'. Assimilation required a fairly high standard of education. It also involved the surrender of native law, adherence to monogamy and sometimes required a period of military service or French employment for at least ten years. It has been estimated that by 1937 out of some 15,000,000 Africans in French West Africa no more than 80,000 had succeeded in acquiring French citizenship. Unlike the British the French had no positive policy, even a slow one, for training their colonial peoples for eventual self-government. Consequently the French were caught unprepared when the desire for self-government swept through West Africa after the Second World War.

German colonial policy and rule

The Germans were greatly handicapped by an almost total lack of experience in dealing with Africans before acquiring their two colonies of Togo and the Cameroons in West Africa. The German colonial administrators in the two colonies acted almost entirely independently. The German colonial governors had advisory councils of nominated German residents. It may be said that up to 1907 the German colonial record had not been a successful one, and the need for reform was recognized by the German Government itself.

In Germany itself there was an efficient bureaucratic system; but this system was autocratic. This was transferred almost wholly to Africa. German colonial administration was not autocratic to Africans alone; it was so also to German residents like missionaries and settlers. In their dealings with the African peoples the Germans displayed an unwillingness to take account of local conditions and this did them no good.

German colonial rule was unsuccessful from the economic point of view also. Things were, however, comparatively better in Togo. Very little private capital entered the German colonies in Africa. Inevitably troubles in the Cameroons and also in German Southwest Africa led to criticism of German colonial rule inside Germany itself. In 1907 a number of changes in German colonial policy were proposed. Colonial matters were taken away from the control of the German Foreign Office and entrusted to a new Colonial Office headed by a very imaginative German imperialist called Dernburg who ordered experiments to find out the best ways of doing things. Dernburg was convinced that German colonization was not going to make any headway unless the German people became more interested in their overseas colonies.

A period of experiments began in 1909. Research stations were established in the German colonies to develop crops and animals. Sociological researches were also conducted. However, the period between 1909 and 1914, when the First World War broke out, was too short for the new changes to make any real impact and besides there was opposition to the changes from old-fashioned German administrators, so that not much was achieved by the end of the German colonial era.

In the peace treaties after the First World War Germany was deprived of her colonies in Africa. In West Africa both Togo and the Cameroons were split between Britain and France. They were not declared outright as British or French colonies but were made mandated territories. Britain and France as mandatory powers were expected to give an account of their stewardship to the League of Nations in respect of both Togo and the Cameroons.

A period of revolutionary changes

The period of colonial rule has usually been viewed in terms of exploitation of the African peoples. This is largely because of the nature of the struggle for independence and of the general feeling against colonialism as a system. However, the objectionable aspects of colonial rule should not hide the fact that the first fifty years or so of the present century mark a period of far-reaching changes in social, economic and technological development: a period which has revolutionized life in West Africa. West Africa, as it were, was pushed into the moving stream of the modern world.

Ironically, the independent states of West Africa are nearly all of them colonial creations. A valid criticism of the colonial boundaries drawn arbitrarily all over West Africa is that they cut across ethnic groups, divided peoples of common heritage, and caused inconvenience and hardship to them. However, what alternative political and national developments might have taken place if events had taken their natural course in the areas occupied by the modern states such as Nigeria, Ghana, the Ivory Coast and Senegal (to mention only a random few) is a subject for speculation far beyond us.

The colonial powers used the early years of the present century to establish their authority and discover the potential wealth of the various territories. The physical problems involved in this process were enormous. Means of transport and communication had to be developed to gain access to the areas with natural resources and also to reach various sections of the population if they were to be effectively ruled. This task was not easy particularly in areas of the rain forest; but gradually some progress was made. Roads were built and the motor lorry, which had been invented in Europe earlier in the century, began to appear on the new roads in West Africa. Railways were constructed, often running from the coast into the interior. By 1930 West Africa could boast of a number of railways. In Nigeria, it was agreed in 1912 that the Lagos–Ibadan line, completed in 1901, be extended to Kano. Between 1913 and 1916 an important line was built in the eastern part of the country to link Port Harcourt and Enugu. Other extensions were soon made. In Ghana a line that had been started from Sekondi in 1898 was extended steadily till it finally reached Kumasi in 1903; and by 1923 a second line linking Kumasi and Accra had been completed. In Sierra Leone the principal railway ran from Freetown, the capital, across to the north-eastern corner of the country. The notable railways in French West Africa are the Dakar-Kayes-Bamako line and that from Abidjan northwards to Wagadugu in Upper Volta. In Togo, Dahomey, the Ivory Coast and Guinea important railways had been built by 1930.

The various railways passed through or led to areas of natural resources and were of great importance in the economic development of the countries they served. Great efforts had been made in the early years of the colonial

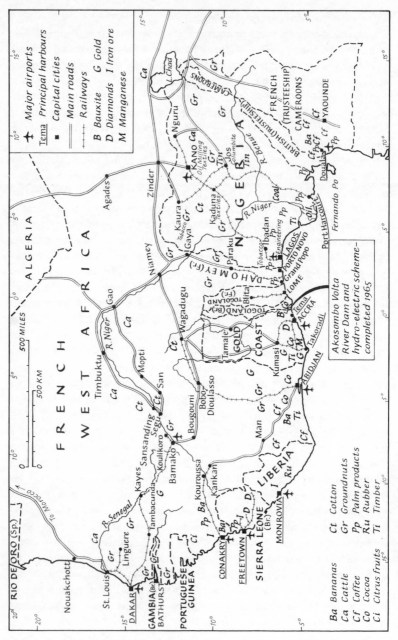

Economic development in West Africa

period to discover mineral deposits and to develop other available resources. Gold, manganese and diamonds were discovered in Ghana. In Nigeria, coal and tin were found. Guinea was found to possess rich deposits of bauxite (not yet fully exploited). Diamonds were discovered in Sierra Leone after the First World War. All these discoveries boosted the economy of the various countries. The production of palm oil, which had been going on for many years in the Ivory Coast, Dahomey and Southern Nigeria, received greater attention. And so did the cultivation of groundnuts in Northern Nigeria, the Gambia, Senegal and the savannah areas of French West Africa. The rain forests were found to contain much valuable hardwood which was felled on an ever-growing scale for timber. The introduction of cocoa made a revolutionary economic change in Ghana and a considerable contribution to the economies of the Ivory Coast, Togo and Western Nigeria. The fact that the production of cocoa was (except in the case of the Ivory Coast) wholly in the hands of local peasant farmers established a class of prosperous indigenous farmers.

The exploitation of mineral and agricultural resources brought profound changes in the lives of the people of West Africa. Before mentioning the most significant of these changes we should note that the overall benefits to West Africa could have been greater. The fact that this was not the case was mainly because the mineral resources were extracted by British and French companies and the lion's share of the gains went to foreign share-holders. The prices of cocoa, palm oil and groundnuts were neither fixed by the African producers nor after negotiation with them: the foreign buyers determined the prices.

Although the new economic activities were controlled by European companies and share-holders, the governments of the various colonial territories derived considerable revenue to run their administrations and to embark upon a number of social services. Sanitary and medical services were provided in the main towns. Postal services were established along the roads and railways. The introduction of the telegraph provided the quickest way of communication. As the administrative services were extended a growing number of West Africans were called upon to work as clerks and similar junior staff. The European commercial firms and houses also offered similar employment opportunities. Besides, large numbers of people were employed in the gold, manganese, tin, coal and diamond mines. The firm establishment of a money economy brought a revolutionary change to life in West Africa. The British introduced a common currency for use in their four colonies; the French did the same throughout French West Africa. The West Africans who sold their services in various ways – in the offices, stores, mines, plantations – received cash payments (usually on a monthly basis) for their services. Cowrie shells and other cumbersome means of exchange of former times (bars of copper or iron, pieces of cloth, for example) disappeared except in very remote areas. The universal use of money meant that, by saving enough money, people could readily obtain what they wanted. This was a most important development.

Expanding facilities for employment meant that large numbers of people left their home areas for the big towns and mining locations. West Africans had always travelled quite extensively: the Hausa, the Fulani and the Dyula were to be found in earlier times far away from their homes. However, there had been nothing like the great labour migrations that took place in various parts of West Africa in the first half of the twentieth century. Men and women of different language and cultural backgrounds found themselves living together in towns and settlements in which outsiders sometimes outnumbered the native population. We cannot go into the sociological effects following this development, but we should note that living in towns and under impersonal urban conditions became the experience of thousands of West Africans who had never experienced this kind of thing before. Large and new towns of mixed populations like Abidjan, Obuasi and Enugu, sprang up. The fact that many workers now moved periodically backwards and forwards between their rural villages and the mining centres and other big towns facilitated the passage of ideas and fashions. Intermarriage and frequent personal contacts helped to break down barriers between various peoples of each country. Migratory labour and the general movement of peoples went on even across the borders of colonial territories.

The growing economic activities of the big towns helped to sustain peoples in remote rural districts. Workers from these areas would make remittances of money from time to time to their families back home.

There was one exciting aspect of the economic changes. This was the new technological experience to which West Africans were exposed in increasing numbers. They found themselves driving motor lorries and trucks and even railway locomotives. They were learning to operate delicate and complex machines in mines and factories. They mastered new trades such as carpentry, masonry, lathe turning and machine repairing. A clerical class of a kind had always existed in those parts of West Africa where Islamic learning prevailed, but now there emerged a large professional class of clerks who earned their living by copying, typing and keeping accounts and records. West Africa was being progressively or, more correctly, violently invaded by all those things happening in the native countries of the colonial masters in Europe – jobs, modes of transportation, style of dressing, food, drink and many other things, some suitable, some not so suitable. The first half of this century witnessed a change perhaps more radical and more fundamental than anything since the coming of the Iron Age in Africa, say two thousand years ago.

Abetifi Presbyterian Church, Ghana, built in 1880   New Church, opened in 1910

Perhaps the most significant of the changes was in formal education. Formal education through the school system has had a long history in parts of West Africa. In Sierra Leone, the Gambia and Ghana it goes back to the early years of the nineteenth century. By the end of that century there were several secondary schools and institutions of secondary education in the three countries mentioned as well as in one or two others such as Southern Nigeria and Senegal. The pioneers of these earlier schools were the Christian churches. Even in the colonial period the churches still continued to shoulder the main responsibility for formal education. This was especially so in the British colonial territories. Gradually the colonial governments in the various territories assumed more and more responsibility for education by establishing government schools in the larger towns and by giving grants-in-aid to the churches for the running of their schools; for the building of classrooms and the payment of the salaries of teachers.

The approach towards the provision of schools in French West Africa was different. In British West Africa the limitation on progress was mainly financial, but the French colonial governments sought to educate just enough colonial youths to meet the requirements of government services. A few of the chosen youths received higher education in France and became Frenchmen in their outlook and way of life to all intents and purposes. We shall hear more of these men in a later chapter. While the missionary bodies in the British territories gave encouragement to the study and development of West African languages, in French West Africa the French language was almost exclusively used as the medium of education. However, French was consequently so well taught that products of the French colonial schools learned to speak near-perfect French. Pidgin English in English-speaking West Africa today has practically no equivalent in French-speaking West Africa.

Although formal education was one of the fundamental developments during the colonial period, nowhere in West Africa were adequate facilities provided. No West African state had above seven to ten per cent of its people literate on the attainment of independence. The main criticism levelled against education in West Africa during and even after independence is that it has largely produced clerks and people prepared to do 'white-collar' jobs. Moreover, the educated West African has lived in two worlds – the world of the former colonial master and that of his native land. His problem is how to take the best of the two worlds and live in the end as a modern but a true African.

Now let us take a quick final look at the changes that have been taking place all over West Africa since the beginning of the present century. This has been perhaps the period of most fundamental changes. Great developments have taken place in the fields of economy, technology, education and social life in general. However, it should be realized that these changes have made their full impact mainly in the towns and urban centres. It is true that nowhere in West Africa do people live exactly as their grandfathers and fathers lived, say, fifty years ago. However, it is also true that in many rural areas the new changes have been slow in registering their effects. Even in many of the areas most affected by the changes the new and the old ways march side by side, sometimes so much so that specimens of West Africa yesterday and West Africa today are readily on show everywhere.

Questions

1. What is indirect rule and how did it work in general?
2. Compare the methods adopted by the British, French and Germans in administering their colonies.
3. Outline the main changes that took place in West Africa during the period of colonial rule and show their importance.

For further reading

Fage, J. D., *A History of West Africa* (pp. 175–98), Cambridge University Press, 1969.
Lugard, F. D., *Amalgamation Report,* 1919.
Ward, W. E. F., *Government in West Africa,* Allen and Unwin, 1965.

12 The road to independence

British West Africa

During the eight years between 1957 and 1965, all the four British colonies in West Africa had won their independence: the Gold Coast which adopted the new name Ghana in 1957, Nigeria in 1960 followed by Sierra Leone in 1961, and the Gambia in 1965. The progress towards this final achievement was a long one. All the four colonies followed a similar pattern of constitutional development although the peculiar circumstances prevailing in each affected the general course of events.

The constitutional pattern up to the period of the First World War was roughly as follows. The governor of each colony was assisted by an Executive Council consisting of a small number of senior officials. This council was essentially an advisory one; the governor consulted it in formulating policy but he was not bound to take its advice. Each colony had a legislative council which helped the governor to make laws. The legislative council developed rather slowly. In the early stages it consisted of a majority of official members and a number of unofficial members usually nominated by the governor. For many years the official members continued to be in the majority. This ensured support for measures introduced by the governor.

The Africans expressed dissatisfaction at their lack of influence in the running of affairs that affected them. In Bathurst, Freetown, Cape Coast, Accra and Lagos, the slow but steady progress of education since the middle of the nineteenth century had produced a number of educated Africans and professional men such as lawyers, doctors and teachers. This class wanted a share in the process of government. They sometimes bitterly opposed measures adopted by the government which they regarded as against their interests. We have seen how the Creoles in Sierra Leone resented measures on the part of the colonial government aimed at reducing their influence. It may also be noted that, even before the end of the nineteenth century, remarkable political activity had begun in the Gold

Coast. In 1897 the Government of the Gold Coast introduced a Lands Bill which was considered by the people and their chiefs as a design to deprive them of their lands. The protest against the Bill led to the formation of the Gold Coast Aborigines Rights Protection Society. It sent a delegation to London to protest against the Bill, and the Colonial Office persuaded the Gold Coast Government to withdraw the Bill in the end. This was a welcome victory for the Aborigines Society (as it came to be called for short) and it continued with vigorous political activity.

Changes after the First World War

The coming of the First World War was something of a surprise and a shock to the peoples of West Africa. The Europeans, when acquiring colonies, had pledged themselves to ensuring peace by stopping wars and hostile and barbaric activities. But now they were fighting a very big war indeed in their own countries; and they were calling upon their colonial subjects to assist them against their enemies! Colonial troops from the Gold Coast overran German forces in Togo and Nigerian troops did the same in the Cameroons. French colonial troops similarly helped their French masters in various fields of the war. All this must have been both puzzling and exciting not only to the colonial troops but also to the African peoples as a whole.

In 1916, while the war was still going on, a new constitution was introduced in the Gold Coast. The number of unofficial members on the legislative council was increased from four to nine. There were to be eleven official members on it. The nine unofficial members were nominated by the governor in this manner: three Europeans, three chiefs and three educated Africans. So all told there were six Africans as against fourteen Europeans. The Aborigines Society attacked the constitution but no immediate changes were made. At this stage, a very significant development took place. The activities of the Aborigines Society developed into a movement aimed at bringing together all the four British West African colonies, thus starting the first pan-African movement in this part of Africa. After the Aborigines Society had failed to secure an improvement in the 1916 constitution, one of its leading members, Mr J. E. Casley Hayford, founded the National Congress of British West Africa in 1917. The aim was to bring the four colonies together in dealing with the British. The Gold Coast was the nerve centre of the Congress but there were branches and influential members in Nigeria, Sierra Leone and the Gambia. The Congress proposed to the British Government that when the war was over a common legislative council should be set up for British West Africa. It also petitioned that African judges and magistrates be appointed. It further proposed the establishment of a university to serve the four colonies.

What came out of all this? It is a matter of regret that the Gold Coast, which had led the way in founding the Congress should have been the occasion for its failure. The Congress sent a delegation to London to press its proposals on the Secretary of State. While the delegation was still in London a group of members of the Aborigines Society cabled a message from the Gold Coast to say that the Gold Coast members on the delegation had no mandate from the chiefs and people of the country. The delegation foundered. The petition was rejected by the Secretary of State and the Congress suffered a severe setback.

In spite of the confusion over the delegation to London and the subsequent failure of the Congress as a pan-African movement, the Aborigines Society continued its political activities at home. It began to press Sir Gordon Guggisberg, who had been appointed governor of the Gold Coast in 1923, to revise the 1916 constitution. Guggisberg was a rare type of colonial governor. He was deeply concerned about progress and he embarked upon significant development projects. He planned expansion in education and founded the famous Achimota College in Accra. To help trade and commerce he built a large harbour at Takoradi. To improve health services he built Korle Bu hospital in Accra. He did other notable things but it is about his constitutional reforms we are immediately concerned. In 1925, in response to demands by the Aborigines Society, Guggisberg introduced a new constitution. Of the 29 members who were now to sit in the legislative council there were 14 unofficial as against 15 official members. The governor could still count on official majority but the Africans now had increased representation. The unofficial members included a number of chiefs. The 1925 constitution also provided for the creation of provincial councils of chiefs. The colonial governments always thought that the chiefs should play a leading role in all constitutional developments. This was to lead to suspicion from the educated people. The 1925 constitution applied only to the Gold Coast Colony; Ashanti and the Northern Territories were governed directly by the governor through chief commissioners.

Similar changes took place elsewhere in British West Africa after the First World War. In Nigeria, which had been united as one country in 1914, a legislative council existed in the Colony of Lagos. In 1922 a new constitution provided for a legislative council of 26 official members and 15 nominated unofficial members. This position prevailed till after the Second World War. In Sierra Leone the legislative council had consisted mainly of official members and not more than two nominated unofficial members till 1923 when the unofficial members were increased to five. However, in 1924 a new constitution provided for 11 official and seven nominated unofficial members. In the Gambia the legislative council consisted of a majority of official members (drawn largely from the advisers to the governor) and one or two unofficial members nominated by the governor.

It will be seen that even in the most advanced of the constitutions there was a majority of official members in the legislative council. The idea was to ensure support to the governor. But the important thing about the steady increase in unofficial members, although always in the minority, is the fact that no sensible colonial governor would totally ignore persistent opinion expressed by the unofficial members who could claim to represent the people and their interests. This was a check of some sort on the action of the governor.

Changes after the Second World War

The war years (1939–45) were uneventful as far as constitutional development was concerned. However, the colonial governors appear to have appreciated the need for constitutional advance as soon as the war was over. The general calm as well as positive support on the part of the colonial peoples towards the war effort deserved recognition as a sign of maturity. As soon as the war ended requests for constitutional reform began in almost all of the four colonies. The general situation was different from what it had been after the First World War. During the Second World War thousands of West African soldiers served with credit in fighting as far away as Burma. A few of them had held positions of considerable responsibility. The soldiers returned home with the experience of men who had seen the wide world. They had learned many new things and formed new ideas. They had acquired confidence in their ability. Moreover, as compared with the situation after the First World War, each of the colonies could now boast of considerable numbers of educated people. The establishment of the Colonial Development and Welfare Fund by the British Government immediately after the Second World War helped to give many young men and women from the British West African colonies further education, not only in academic subjects but also in technical and industrial fields. This made available increased personnel for positions of responsibility in administration, commerce and industry. It was in such circumstances that post-war constitutional reforms were embarked upon. At this stage it may be useful to examine the outlines of the changes that took place in each colony until final independence was won.

The Gold Coast

Sir Alan Burns was appointed governor of the Gold Coast in 1942 while the war was going on. In 1946, that is shortly after the war, he proposed a new constitution for the country. In many respects the new constitution was a great step forward. In the new legislature there was to be a majority of elected members representing the people. The elected members outnumbered the official members and the nominated members together; and for the first time members from Ashanti and the Northern Territories were to sit in the legislative council.

The 1946 constitution, however, had inherent weaknesses which made it unacceptable to the practised politicians. Dr J. B. Danquah described it as 'window dressing', much to the annoyance of Sir Alan Burns. Quite apart from the fact that under the new constitution the governor was armed with the power to veto or refuse to accept a decision by the legislature if he thought it necessary so to do, the unofficial majority in the legislative council had no positive power. They could neither propose legislation nor initiate policy. They had no control over the executive; the executive council which now had on it three Africans, was not accountable to the legislature. In short the unofficial majority could criticize and offer opinion; they could not initiate or control policy. But as duly elected representatives of the people their voice could not be lightly dismissed.

The short-comings of the 1946 constitution led to widespread political activity as never before known in the country. The post-war difficulties and the great expectations of the people as well as growing national consciousness helped political activity. All sections of the people were aroused and involved in a political reawakening. In 1947 Dr J. B. Danquah and others founded the United Gold Coast Convention (the U.G.C.C.), the first real mass political movement, to press for further constitutional reform that would give the people self-government. Branches were opened all over the country. In February 1948 widespread riots occurred in the Gold Coast which had hitherto been regarded as the most loyal and indeed a model colony. There had been a month-long boycott of European goods throughout the country in protest against rising prices. The day the boycott ended coincided with the shooting and killing of three ex-servicemen in a group marching to Government House to present a petition to the governor. Looting and rioting started spontaneously in Accra and spread quickly to other big towns. The new governor, Sir Gerald Creasy, panicked and arrested Dr Danquah and Dr Nkrumah and four other leaders of the United Gold Coast Convention. A Commission of Inquiry (the Watson Commission) was set up to investigate the causes of the disturbances. The Commission in its final report blamed the troubles mainly on inadequate political responsibility for the people of the Gold Coast.

As a result of the findings of the Watson Commission an All-African Constitutional Committee headed by Sir Henley Coussey, a judge, was appointed to make recommendations for a new constitution. The 1951 constitution for the Gold Coast was the final outcome. There was to be a Legislative Assembly of 75 elected members and 9 nominated members including 3 senior European officials. The governor was to choose a group of ministers from the Assembly to form the executive. The Executive Council was still to be responsible to the governor who continued to be armed with reserve powers – the veto.

Shortly after the Watson Commission, Dr Kwame Nkrumah, the General Secretary of the United Gold Coast Convention, broke away to form his own party, the Convention Peoples Party (the C.P.P.). A large number of the members of the U.G.C.C. joined Nkrumah's new party. But the U.G.C.C., though weakened by defections, still functioned under the leadership of Dr Danquah. Its slogan 'Self-Government in the shortest possible time', did not appeal to the people as did the C.P.P's 'Self-Government NOW!' In 1951 general elections were held under the new constitution while Nkrumah was serving a prison sentence for disturbing the peace. His party, however, won overwhelmingly and he himself was returned with a vast majority for a seat in Accra.

The governor, Sir Charles Arden-Clerk, sent for Nkrumah from jail to form a government. The cabinet was made up of eight African ministers and three ex-officio British ministers in charge of finance, justice and external affairs. Nkrumah was given the title Leader of Government Business, but in 1952 was recognized and styled Prime Minister. Although the Gold Coast was not yet fully independent it now enjoyed self-government; it had control of its internal affairs.

The next few years before final independence were eventful years for the country. Nkrumah's C.P.P. Government was determined to carry out the promises it had made to the people concerning development in general. And notable changes did take place. Roads were built; an accelerated development programme in education was launched. Everywhere there were visible signs of progress. But there was growing discontent against Nkrumah's government. It rode rough-shod over its political opponents. It favoured party functionaries, and stories of corruption and nepotism were circulated against it. Nkrumah showed open disregard for the chiefs who felt their traditional authority seriously threatened. The centralization of power by the C.P.P., firmly based in the south of the country, alarmed people in the regions, especially in Ashanti. The fear of over-centralization aided by a reduction in cocoa price by Nkrumah's government touched off a strong national movement in Ashanti in opposition to the C.P.P. – the National Liberation Movement (the N.L.M.). At the same time another regional party emerged in the Northern Territories, the Northern Peoples Party, led by the chiefs. The fear of 'creeping dictatorship' under the C.P.P. firmly established in the south made the N.L.M. adopt secession as a war cry.

In July 1956 the last elections before independence were held amidst great tension. The C.P.P. again won the elections convincingly. The British Government had pledged to grant independence if requested by a reasonable majority in the new Legislative Assembly. Nkrumah commanded such a majority. After a period of compromise a final constitution for independence was agreed upon and in March 1957 the Gold Coast became the independent state of Ghana within the Commonwealth.

Nigeria

In 1946 Nigeria was given a new constitution which, like that of the Gold Coast in the same year, provided for a legislature with a majority of elected members. Again as in the case of the Gold Coast the new legislature consisted of members from all the three regions of Nigeria sitting together for the first time. Regional councils were set up in the North, the West and the East to facilitate administration. Among other things the regional councils could examine estimates and bills before they were tabled in the legislature at Lagos. They acted, however, in an advisory capacity and their powers were limited.

In 1951 further changes were introduced in the constitution, similar to those in the Gold Coast the same year. The central legislature in Lagos had 142 members, nearly all of them elected by the regional assemblies. The Executive Council was made responsible to the legislature. In 1954 Nigeria formally became a federation with Regional Governments in the North, the West and the East with a Federal Government in Lagos. The powers reserved

Kano

to the Federal Government were spelt out in the constitution but those for the Regional Governments were not specifically listed. 1954 marked the beginning of a period of great competition among the three Regions for rapid development. Roads were built and rapid expansion in education took place.

Political parties played an important part in bringing about independence in Nigeria as in the Gold Coast. The parties in Nigeria tended to be regional. The dominant peoples in the North, the West and the East were Hausa-Fulani, Yoruba and Ibo respectively. Three main parties emerged in the regions with massive local support: the Northern Peoples Congress in the North led by Sir Amadu Bello, the Saudana of Sokoto; the Action Group under Mr Obafemi Awolowo in the West; and the National Council of Nigeria and the Cameroons (the N.C.N.C.) under Dr Nnamdi Azikiwe in the East. The nature of the political parties created a problem about control of the Federal Parliament. As the Northern Region was larger than the West and the East put together, the Northern Peoples Congress was in a position to dominate the Federal Parliament. But this situation was averted when, after elections in 1960, the N.C.N.C. (now standing not for National Council of Nigeria and the Cameroons but for the National Council of Nigerian Citizens, the Southern Cameroons having decided to break away from Nigeria to join the French Cameroons) joined the Northern Peoples Congress in forming a coalition government on the attainment of independence by Nigeria. Dr Azikiwe then left politics and became the first Governor-General of independent Nigeria. Sir Abubakar Tafawa Balewa of the Northern Peoples Congress was the Prime Minister. The Action Group became the federal opposition, with Mr Awolowo as leader of the opposition in the Federal House of Representatives.

Sierra Leone

The 1924 constitution was operated without any significant changes till 1953 when the membership of the legislative council was increased to thirty. There were seven ex-officio members as against twenty-one elected representatives from the Colony and the Protectorate. Thus in 1953 Sierra Leone, like the Gold Coast and Nigeria two years earlier, got an unofficial majority in the legislature. The Executive Council consisted of five ex-officio members and six elected members chosen by the governor. They were soon styled as ministers.

In July 1954 Dr Milton Margai, leader of the Sierra Leone Peoples' Party he had founded in 1951, became Chief Minister. His party had swept the polls in 1953 over his rival Dr Bankole Bright's National Council of Sierra Leone. Dr Margai's party derived its strength mainly from the Protectorate while Dr Bright's party was mainly based in the Colony. In 1956 the legislature became known as the House of Representatives. In 1958 further changes were made in the constitution. The ex-officio members were removed from the House of Representatives and the number of elected members was increased. The governor still presided over the Executive Council but now all its members were drawn from the House of Representatives. The governor had reserve powers over defence, external affairs and internal security and the police.

In 1961 the last limitations were removed from the constitution and Sierra Leone became completely independent.

The Gambia

There was little change in the 1902 constitution till after the Second World War. The steps taken towards constitutional reform in the Gambia were rather cautious. A significant change occurred in 1954 when an enlarged legislative council consisted of a majority of unofficial members. The Executive Council was reformed to consist of four ex-officio members and six members appointed from among the elected members of the legislative council. The members of the Executive were soon styled as ministers. In 1961 the House of Representatives was enlarged, and the constitution was modified in 1962. In 1963 the Executive Council became the cabinet, led by a Prime Minister. In that year the Gambia obtained internal self-government. In 1965 the final stage was reached when the Gambia became fully independent.

The position of chiefs

There has always been the tradition of powerful chieftaincies in all the four English-speaking countries of West Africa. We have already discussed the most important kingdoms in this area. The British recognized the power and influence of the chiefs and employed it under the system of indirect rule. The various colonial governments were of the view that constitutional development should centre round the chiefs: hence the appointment of chiefs to the legislative councils and the setting up of provincial councils for chiefs. But invariably the up-and-coming generation of educated men looked upon the reliance on the chiefs by the colonial authorities with disfavour and suspicion.

The colonial governors thought that as the chiefs had always been the effective rulers of their peoples in the past it was only wise to nurture and take advantage of their position in any new forms of government and administrative arrangements that would be introduced. But the educated class of West Africans was quick to point out that for the chiefs to sit side by side with their subjects on legislative councils where the chiefs were expected to express their opinion without prior consultation with their elders was contrary to custom. The chiefs were the fathers of their peoples.

They should sit back for their children to come to them for advice. Moreover, the business of modern administration and government was so complicated that it was feared that unless they were reasonably educated the chiefs were likely to be duped by European officials. The insistence of the colonial governors on using the chiefs in the legislative councils, although sincere, created suspicion among the educated people who said that the chiefs were being used as tools by the colonial governments. Whether this was so or not the suspicion grew apace until the chiefs began to lose prestige. This made it difficult for them to play the role the British administrators had planned for them in constitutional development. But all this is not to say that the chiefs actually failed their subjects. Some of them were able spokesmen for their people in the legislative councils. Some of them served creditably in defence of the rights of their people. We have seen how the chiefs of the Gold Coast joined their educated subjects in protesting against the Lands Bill of 1897.

The emergence of political parties led by non-chiefs reduced the standing of the chiefs before their subjects. Those chiefs who supported the new political parties and identified themselves with them found themselves in the end playing second fiddle in the new power politics. Those chiefs who expressed apathy or opposition to the political parties only earned scorn and ridicule. Nkrumah of Ghana threatened the chiefs that they were no problem and that they would 'run away and leave their sandals'.

The political parties were generally strong and most vocal in the big towns and the urban centres. The influence of the chiefs in these areas waned. Where municipal and town councils operated, the chiefs lost to these councils some of their former responsibilities. In the rural areas, however, the chiefs by and large remained the effective rulers and fathers of their people in the daily affairs of life.

The progressive development of European-style government gradually undermined the traditional authority of the chiefs. One of the problems in post-independence West Africa is how to regulate the relation between the traditional authority of chiefs and the new democratic principles based upon popular vote. Nowhere have the chiefs been openly denounced yet. Everywhere they seem to be recognized at least as the 'repositories of African culture'.

French West Africa

We saw in the last chapter that while Britain entertained the idea that one day in the distant future its African colonies would become independent, the French did not think that way. The French policy was gradually to turn the colonial peoples into French citizens. The French were so confident about the superiority of their civilization and culture that they did not see anything odd about this policy. Their system of education in the colonies was geared towards achieving this policy.

The uncertainties and the compelling social and economic problems which showed themselves in West Africa after the Second World War revealed the inherent weakness in the policy of 'Frenchifying' the colonial peoples. The peoples of French West Africa could not fail to be influenced by the constitutional changes that were introduced in British West Africa from the mid-1940s.

After 1945 the French instituted for the benefit of their colonial peoples in West Africa a programme of education and development similar to those offered by the British through the Colonial Development and Welfare Fund. This reinforced a development that had been going on for some time. The very Africans who had received the best that French education and civilization could offer, people like Leopold Senghor of Senegal and Houphouet-Boigny of the Ivory Coast, began to express admiration and hanker after things essentially African. As we have already seen Leopold Senghor was a leading exponent of Négritude. Négritude stressed that there was as much in African civilization as any other. In political terms it meant that the African was good enough and possessed enough resources to enable him to reassert himself and be free to control his own destiny. Such ideas would not fit into the French policy of turning colonial peoples into Frenchmen. To put it briefly, the growing national feeling in West Africa after the Second World War was bound to upset the French colonial system and policy. The French were badly shaken as they had not prepared themselves for such a development. The British knew that it would happen and were expecting it, even if only in the distant future.

The Constituent Assembly and after

The French Government had planned that when the Second World War was over a Constituent Assembly would be held to work out ties between France and her colonial peoples. A French Union embodying France and the colonies was envisaged.

In 1945 the proposed Constituent Assembly took place. A new constitution proposed among other things that all Africans were to be given full French citizenship; the old system of compulsory labour was to be abolished in the colonies; the excessive and arbitrary use of power by administrators was to be curtailed. The provisions of the constitution were approved in 1946. Each of the eight French West African colonies was given a territorial assembly. There was to be a Great Council for the whole group in Dakar. A number of Africans were elected to the French National Assembly in Paris. But all this did not kill the emergence of nationalist feeling to which we have referred. In October 1946 a conference of the African members of the Constituent Assembly was held in Bamako. The French Government had become alarmed about the possible outcome of the conference and did all it could to dissuade members from attending. Senghor was prevailed upon to stay away from the conference. But the conference did take place as planned and the main result was the formation of a political party known as the Rassemblement Démocratique Africaine (the R.D.A.). Houphouet-Boigny of the Ivory Coast became the leader of the R.D.A. When the next general elections to the French National Assembly were held, the R.D.A. was able to return several members to it. The party then made a tactical mistake and thereby played into the hands of the French Government by allying itself with the French Communist Party. However, Houphouet-Boigny quickly realized the danger and began to work to bring the alliance to an end.

The French Government deeply distrusted the R.D.A. and used all possible means to weaken it, although Houphouet-Boigny did his best to co-operate with the Government. In 1950 serious riots occurred at Dimbokro in the Ivory Coast and the French Government used this as an excuse to ban all R.D.A. meetings in the French West African territories. But when colonial governments begin to do this kind of thing they only help to strengthen the nationalist feeling they set out to destroy.

In the 1950s France was faced with serious troubles in Indo-China leading finally to the collapse of French rule in that part of the Far East and resulting in the establishment of the three separate and independent states of Laos, Cambodia and Viet Nam. The French Government began to realize the need for constitutional reform in the remaining colonies.

In 1956 Houphouet-Boigny and several of the R.D.A. were returned to the French National Assembly. Houphouet-Boigny was made a member of the French Cabinet. The most important development in this Assembly was the passing of a new measure known as the *loi-cadre* (outline law) which provided for constitutional reform. Subsequently each of the French West African colonies was given a legislative assembly with control over its domestic affairs.

De Gaulle – Yes or No?

In 1958 General Charles de Gaulle became Prime Minister and in 1959 President of France. Under his constitution for the Fifth French Republic it was proposed to set up a French Community that placed the relationship between France and her colonies on a similar footing to that existing in the British Commonwealth. The territories were free to elect or reject to belong to the Community. But De Gaulle made it clear that any territory which opted out would cease to benefit from French aid in any form. When the day of decision came, all the territories voted 'YES' except Guinea under Sekou Touré which returned a 'NO'. France quickly removed all her personnel and even office equipment from Guinea. But for a loan promptly offered by Ghana, Guinea would have found itself in serious difficulties.

Independence was in sight for the rest of French West Africa. Senegal, Sudan, Dahomey and Upper Volta decided to form a federation under the name Mali. In the end however the Mali Federation consisted only of Sudan and Senegal. But the federation soon disintegrated. Senegal broke away anc Sudan retained the name Mali. The other territories also asked for independence and got it in 1960. Thus ended French West Africa. However all the former colonies except Guinea still maintain a special relationship with France.

Questions

1. Why were the demands for constitutional progress intensified in British West Africa after the Second World War?
2. Take any one colony in British West Africa and show how it moved towards independence after the Second World War.
3. What have been the main difficulties in giving the chiefs a prominent place in the new governments of West Africa.
4. How did French West Africa as a whole move towards independence?

For further reading

Ward, W. E. F., *Government in West Africa*, Allen and Unwin, 1965.
Emergent Africa, Allen and Unwin, 1967.

13 After independence

Social and economic development

The 1960s, the decade of independence in West Africa, was very exciting and crucial. There was a burning desire everywhere for development and progress. During the struggle for independence great pains were taken to show how little the colonial governments had done for their colonies and how much more would be achieved when control of affairs passed into the hands of the sons of the land. After independence rapid development was thus necessary to fulfil the pledges made and the promises held out during the campaign for freedom. But quite apart from this consideration there was everywhere a sincere desire on the part of the rulers of the new states for development so as to catch up as fast as possible with the advanced countries of the world. A leader of one of the newly independent West African states is reported to have told a European ex-colonial officer: 'We have to achieve in twenty years what it took your country a hundred years to do. Time is against us'. However, the enthusiasm to achieve rapid results was matched by the seriousness of the problems involved. Capital for development was short; qualified personnel were lacking or inadequate, and technical know-how had to be procured from outside. But these problems not withstanding poverty, ignorance and disease had to be removed.

Each West African state as it attained independence drew up a development plan spread over a period of time, usually five years. The plans ranged from modest ones to very ambitious ones, such as those of Nigeria, Ghana and the Ivory Coast which made provision for costly projects like big hydro-electric schemes. Every state wanted to do its utmost for its peoples.

Three main sources were available to the newly independent states for financing development projects: revenue raised internally, loans and aid from foreign countries and international agencies and organizations, and foreign investment. Few of the states had at the time of independence enough internal revenue to carry out the projects they had planned for development. But fortunately almost all of them had attained independence

Akosombo hydroelectric generating station, Ghana

amidst universal goodwill. The former colonial powers were usually willing to be of assistance in development. They were ready to give technical assistance and to grant loans on favourable terms. Besides, Agencies of the United Nations Organization such as UNESCO (United Nations Educational, Scientific and Cultural Organization), FAO (Food and Agricultural Organization), WHO (World Health Organization) and also the World Bank and the International Monetary Fund were prepared to offer assistance. But the demands upon the resources of these international agencies were so extensive as to limit what they could do for any one country. Foreign investment has thus become an important factor in the economy of the developing countries. As a rule, however, investors are shrewd and rather cautious about undertaking risks. It is usually the countries with considerable economic potential and stable political conditions that are able to attract foreign capital. From all this it will be seen that the great enthusiasm for development on the part of the new states of West Africa could be dampened by lack of funds. And yet everywhere considerable development has taken place since independence.

One of the first things that engaged the attention of a number of the new states was the improvement of transport and communication. This was essential to facilitate movement of peoples and to promote economic activity. However, in many parts of West Africa much still remains to be done in providing roads and railways. In some areas foodstuffs are held up in the rural areas because of lack of feeder roads.

The governments of the various states were all deeply committed to raising the standard of living of their peoples. Pledges and promises had been made to do this during the period immediately before independence. Much of the social services available during the colonial period had been concentrated in the big towns and urban centres. The rural areas were generally poor. There was a crying need for clean water, sanitary and medical services and for schools. Attention was given to all these in a serious way immediately after independence. The degree of achievement has varied from state to state depending upon the available resources. Considerable progress has been made in the richer states; in the not-so-rich ones a useful start has been made. But it will take years and vast sums of money to bridge the gap in social services between the urban centres and the rural areas throughout West Africa. The greatest drawback to the extension of medical services in all the states has been the acute shortage of doctors. There has been awareness of this situation. Even before independence Nigeria had tried to solve the problem by establishing a faculty of medicine at the University of Ibadan. Shortly after independence a medical school was started in Lagos, the federal capital. Ghana soon followed suit and set up a faculty of medicine at the University of Ghana in Legon, Accra. Even so in these two countries there are still not enough doctors to cope with the medical needs of the people.

For some time now there has been a steady and ever-increasing movement of people from the rural areas to the towns and cities throughout West Africa. One result of this development has been an acute shortage of housing. Growing slums and shanty suburbs are the common features of most West African cities. Governments have been aware of this and where funds are available quite impressive schemes for housing estates have been put into operation. In Ibadan, Lagos, Accra, Enugu, Kumasi and Abidjan considerable progress has been made in this respect.

Each independent state of West Africa has given priority to education. The development plan for each country made special provision for the expansion of educational facilities. Some states have moved faster than others, depending upon the available resources. Ghana, for example, offers free tuition up to the secondary school level for all for whom places can be found in the schools. The education budget accounts for about a quarter of the total revenue of the country. Other countries are making similar efforts. Nigeria has opened three new universities since independence. The Ivory Coast has established its own university in Abidjan. Dahomey is currently

Aerial view of Accra

General view of Freetown, showing Parliament Building in the middle distance

New secondary school buildings, Ghana

planning for one. In some states the number of pupils in schools has doubled or increased significantly since independence. In countries such as Ghana and Nigeria commendable efforts have been made in adult education. Efforts to make grown-up people literate, at least in their mother tongues, are reinforced by courses in hygiene and sanitation, diet, housekeeping and birth control and care of children. But in recent years there has been one serious question facing nearly all the independent states of West Africa concerning expansion of formal education. This is how to find employment for the thousands of boys and girls who leave school each year.

One important aspect of economic development in West Africa since independence has been industrialization. In colonial times economic activity was centred on agriculture and the production of raw materials to feed the industries of the colonial powers. Although the rulers of the various states have recognized the importance of introducing modern techniques into agriculture they have been anxious to diversify the economies of their countries through industrialization. Reliance on a single major cash crop such as cocoa in Ghana has long been rightly recognized as risky. A fall in the world price of a principal commodity could lead to economic disaster. It has moreover been felt that industrialization would create opportunities for employment while reducing reliance on imported manufactured goods. Efforts were therefore made soon after independence to establish industries in a number of West African states. Achievement in this respect has depended upon the potential resources of the states and

Cocoa nursery, Sierra Leone

Cocoa processing factory, Lagos

Loading timber, Ghana

other relevant factors. There have been difficulties. Supply of raw materials has not always been steady or cheap. There have been delays in procuring essential spare parts for machinery. Managerial skill has not always been commendable. Dishonesty and corruption have impeded progress and production. There have been cases of industrial projects not properly conceived, or set up with an eye to national prestige rather than to their real usefulness. Foreign countries entering into contracts for industrial development in West African countries have been known to take undue advantage and have seen to their own gains at the expense of their African partners or clients. Unserviceable machinery is believed to have been reconditioned and palmed off on West African state governments. Foreign technical personnel have demanded exorbitant salaries and extremely favourable conditions of service. All this has had telling effects on efforts to set up and develop industries. All the same reasonable progress has been made in a number of states. Nigeria and Ghana have successful textile and steel industries. The Ivory Coast boasts of soap and vegetable oil industries firmly based on locally produced raw materials. Ghana has an aluminium smelter and factory at Tema which produces a number of aluminium products both for the home market and for export. Nigeria and Ghana again have oil refineries and truck assembling plants. There is a whole host of essential commodities now locally manufactured in West Africa: matches, iron rods, hatchets, cigarettes, shoes, sugar, tyres and many others. It may take some time before goods made in West Africa can successfully compete

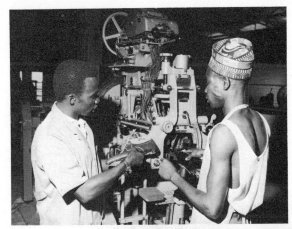

Shoe-making
in Kano

Canning factory,
Kano

Textile factory,
Kano

Cocoa House, Ibadan –
Nigeria's tallest building

in the world market but a necessary step has been taken. Already thousands of people are employed in the industries that have been set up in the various states.

One last word before we leave the question of economic development in West Africa. This is about the gradual realization of the need for inter-state co-operation in economic planning and development. We saw in the last chapter that France made provision for an overall administrative structure for her eight colonies in West Africa with headquarters for the unit in Dakar, Senegal. Britain did not treat her four colonies in this way but even so these colonies enjoyed some common services. There was a British West African Currency Board, a West African Airways Corporation, a West African Cocoa Research Institute serving Nigeria and Ghana in particular, a West African Court of Appeal, and a West African Exaninations Council. All these common services, with the exception of the last mentioned, came to an end on independence. There may have been good reasons for the stoppage, but in recent times the need for co-operation in economic matters at least has come to the fore. The French-speaking states have moved faster in this direction and taken concrete steps. They have set up the organization called OCAM (consisting of the Ivory Coast, Togo, Dahomey, Niger

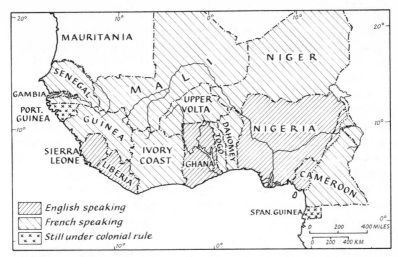

West Africa in 1965

and Upper Volta) which aims at co-ordinating economic planning and development for the member states. Senegal, Mali and Guinea have also been discussing the formation of a Senegal River Organization aimed at utilizing the resources of the Senegal River. There are current negotiations between Ghana, Togo and Dahomey to share electricity produced by the Akosombo dam in Ghana. These measures for co-operation are in the right direction. Unnecessary duplication of services and utilities in each state is a sheer dissipation of resources. Co-operation can lead to saving of capital. Economic co-operation will further promote political union which is one of the future aims of most independent states in Africa.

Political problems
There are some fourteen independent states in West Africa. There have been military take-overs in no less than half of these states and attempted coups in two or three others. This situation tells a story. All has not been well with the political life of West Africa since independence. What are the main problems?

We have made brief reference to the fact that political stability depended upon how well the Westminster type of government adopted by the former British colonies was operated. This type of government is based on the party system. The party with a majority of representatives in the state legislature forms the Government, the other party or group of parties form the Opposition. The success of this arrangement depends greatly on tolerance and a spirit of give and take by both the ruling party and the others that form the

Opposition. Britain and the other countries of the world that have made a success of this type of government have reached their present situation after a long period of experiment. The teething troubles with the system in West Africa have been many and quite disturbing. Let us examine a few of the problems.

Firstly, the tolerance and spirit of give and take mentioned already have not been forthcoming between the Government and Opposition parties. A learned Minister of State declared in a House of Assembly: 'The Government does not share the privilege of ruling this country with the Opposition'. The Government parties in West Africa have tended to regard it as a mark of weakness to give in to the Opposition even when the Opposition has made a valid case. Mistrust on the part of the Government party breeds further mistrust from the Opposition and in the end the relationship and atmosphere become so poisoned that opposition is often regarded as treason.

Secondly, there has been an undue tendency by ruling parties to pamper their followers and supporters by offering them favours which non-supporters are denied. Party functionaries are given jobs and responsibilities for which they may not be qualified – 'jobs for the boys' this practice has been called. The preferential treatment is sometimes carried to the extent of denying districts and areas voting for Opposition candidates developments showered upon areas that have returned members of the ruling parties. Naturally this causes discontent.

Thirdly, political parties have tended to follow the ethnic divisions of a country. The 'home boy' is always right and must be supported. National issues are blurred by local and parochial considerations. This makes difficult the process of nation-building which all governments in the new states of West Africa have declared to be their goal.

Fourthly, the Opposition parties themselves have not always behaved responsibly. Just as the ruling parties regard it as weakness to give in to the Opposition even in good cases, the Opposition parties sometimes fail to support what is clearly a wise government policy in the national interest. The Opposition is often negatively critical. The generally small size of Opposition parties in West Africa breeds a sense of insecurity. The mammoth size of ruling parties on the other hand creates undue confidence and a false sense of security.

Fifthly, the leaders and parties who were in the vanguard of the struggle for independence have tended to claim a perpetual right to rule for as long as they live. Such leaders see any attempt on the part of a section of their people to replace them with new rulers as a mark of ingratitude. They may have acquired a unique atmosphere around them over a period of years, a 'charisma' as it is called, which makes them equate themselves with the

traditional African chief whose authority is not assailed by periodic con-
firmation such as is implied in general elections. All manner of African
traditions have been used in the attempt to enhance and perpetuate the rule
of party political leaders. But the point is that the party system, the appeal
for votes, and the whole concept of electing representatives periodically
cannot leave the old traditions intact.

Lastly, behind all the problems lies the fundamental fact that for party
politics to succeed and the Westminster type of government to be fair and
meaningful, there must be a voting public that can appreciate national issues
and formulate an opinion and press it upon the rulers. It has been too easy
for politicians in West Africa to have their way with the electorate.

The difficulties and problems outlined above did create in a number of
West African states a situation in which the Opposition was forced under-
ground. Harrassed and hunted by high-handed measures by the ruling
party the Opposition may resort to the only avenue left for a change of
government – subversion and violence. It is this that partly accounts for the
many military takeovers that have occurred in West Africa. A successful
coup in one country offers temptation and encouragement for that illegal
and unconstitutional method of changing a government in other countries.

The Organization of African Unity

The emergence of national feeling all over Africa after the Second World
War was accompanied by a Pan-Africa movement, in other words the feeling
that Africa should act together on vital matters. The first Pan-Africa conference was actually held in 1945, the very year the war came to an end, in
Manchester, England. A permanent secretariat was set up. From then onwards the feeling grew apace that one day Africa would be united in some
sort of way. Some even thought at this early stage that one day Africa could
have a Union Government. Dr Kwame Nkrumah who became secretary of
the permanent office was later to spearhead the movement for African unity.

When Ghana became independent in 1957, Nkrumah declared that the
independence of his country was meaningless unless it was linked with the
total liberation of Africa. The following year he called a conference in Accra
of delegates from the eight independent African states at the time. The
liberation of the rest of Africa still under foreign domination was the main
topic discussed by the Accra Conference. But at that stage Nkrumah must
have dropped hints about some form of African unity in the future. African
unity in general terms was an ideal shared by a number of Africanists, that
is, people specially devoted to things purely African.

When Guinea became independent in very difficult circumstances Nkrumah rushed to its help with a substantial loan. Nkrumah was eventually able
to get Guinea and Mali to join Ghana in what became the Ghana-Guinea-

Mali Union. The union did not become very successful in practical terms but Nkrumah then made the union of the whole Africa one of his major pre-occupations. He put forward proposals for a Union Government for Africa to be served by a Military High Command. But although many African leaders saw the need for close co-operation and ultimate unity, the setting up of a Union Government was considered premature. There were some practical difficulties that needed to be taken into consideration.

Firstly, Africa is a vast continent with a great variety of peoples and their particular ways of doing things. It has enormous problems of communication.

Secondly, there were serious differences in the political arrangements and ideas of the various independent states. Some had adopted the parliamentary form of government based on a multi-party system. Some had one-party governments headed by presidents with supreme powers. What form would the Union Government take? This was by no means insurmountable but it needed careful thought. It may be mentioned that by 1962 a number of independent African states had aligned themselves in two loose groups. First, there was the Monrovia Group which consisted of states which although committed to pan-Africanism wanted to see its programmes and aims achieved through moderate means. Then there was on the other hand the Casablanca Group representing the radical states that urged revolutionary methods in solving the problems of the day.

Thirdly, although Nkrumah had himself declared that his Ghana was prepared to surrender its independence 'Wholly or in part', in the interest of African Unity it was not clear whether the other African states were prepared to go as far as this. Coming fresh from colonial rule, many independent states would naturally tend to be jealous of their newly-won independence and would be wary of surrendering it to a new body, as Nkrumah's Ghana was willing to do.

Fourthly, jealousies and rivalries were likely to come up in even secondary issues like choosing the Union capital and the first president and so on. There were other problems but the important thing is that Nkrumah's ideas on Africa Unity were felt to be rather hasty.

It was generally recognized that there was the need for the states of Africa to come together and speak with one voice and take common action on some important international issues. If they could take a common stand at the United Nations, for example, the African states could be a force to reckon with. All this was clear but there was the common feeling that it would be wise 'to hasten slowly'. After intensive diplomatic consultations the heads of independent African states assembled in Addis Ababa in 1963 and the Organization of African Unity was set up. It fell far short of what Nkrumah had wanted: no Union Government was established. What was set up was a Consultative Council on the lines of the Organization of American states. The aims of the O.A.U. were set out in a charter of the Organization.

First and foremost the member states pledged themselves to co-operate in political, economic and other fields. An economic Commission was to be set up in due course to encourage and co-ordinate economic development in various states.

Secondly, the Organization was to resist and eliminate exploitation and interference in the affairs of the African states from outside. This special danger and threat to the true independence of African states has been generally called neo-colonialism. The O.A.U. was to be on the lookout for the slightest signs of neo-colonialism on the continent of Africa. All African states suscribing to the O.A.U. Charter were to avoid becoming tools and agents of neo-colonialism.

Thirdly, the O.A.U. was to give active support to those territories and peoples of Africa not yet free to manage their own affairs such as those in Rhodesia and South Africa. Africans in the Portuguese territories of Mozambique and Angola in central and southern Africa, and in Portuguese Guinea in West Africa were to be supported in their struggle for freedom. Portugal has always regarded these three territories under its rule as extensions of Portugal overseas. It will therefore not hear of independence for them. In all three territories nationalist movements known as Freedom Fighters have been engaged in military action against Portuguese forces for some years. The O.A.U. pledged its aid and support for these nationalists.

One further important aim of the O.A.U. is to try to promote peace on the continent by settling any disputes that may arise between member states to avoid dangerous conflicts. It became clear to the founders of the O.A.U. that before the Organization could speak with an effective voice in world affairs it must set its own house in order. Immediately after its formation the O.A.U. settled down to active business. A General Secretary was appointed and a secretariat was set up. A number of committees and sub-committees were established to deal with specific problems. Economic problems and aid for liberation movements were given special attention. Addis Ababa was finally selected as headquarters of the Organization. Regular annual summit meetings by heads of states were provided for. Such meetings were to take place in the capitals of various states as were decided upon. There were also to be regular meetings by Foreign Ministers of member states.

What has the Organization of African Unity achieved so far? Too much has been expected from the O.A.U. Obviously as a continental body, and given its circumstances, there is a limit to what it can do. It has set up committees which deal with various matters – political matters, economic affairs, aid to freedom fighters in dependent territories. The fact that, in spite of serious differences of opinion, the Organization still holds together is an achievement. Moreover, to its credit it has helped to settle border disputes among member states (such as between Morocco and Algeria and Somalia and Ethiopia) which could have sparked off violent conflicts. It has been trying to mobilize world opinion on questions like apartheid in South Africa and the illegal régime in Rhodesia. It tried hard to mediate between the two warring sides during the Nigerian Civil War. The O.A.U. commands attention in the United Nations, the Secretary-General of which has been present on occasions at the annual conferences of the heads of states and governments in Africa.

Questions

1. Describe the steps taken by any one country in West Africa to improve her economy since independence.
2. What have been the main drawbacks to the rapid development of industries in West Africa?
3. Why has the practice of democracy been difficult in independent West African States?
4. What are the problems in the way of effective African Unity?
5. What are the main aims of the O.A.U.? How far have they been achieved?

For further reading

Post, K., *The New States of West Africa*, Penguin Books, 1964.

Index

Porto Novo, 8, 83, 86, 123
Pra River, 68
Prempeh I (also Kwaku Duah III),
29, 71

Qadriyya, 22
Quaker, Rev. James, 44

Rabeh, 35
Rassemblement Democratique
Africaine (R.D.A.), 148
Rattray, Captain, 126
Recaptives, 42–43
Republican Party (of Liberia), 54
Roberts, Joseph Jenkins, 53
Royal Niger Company, 114–116
Roye, E. J., 54, 55
Rufisque, 59

Sabongari, 15
Sahara, 4
St Louis (Senegal), 59, 128
Samori Toure, career of, 25–31, 47,
122
Sanankoro, 25
Segu, 8, 21
Seif dynasty, 32, 34
Seku Almadu, 21–22
Select Committee of 1865, 49, 77,
107, 122
Sene-Gambia, 6, 10
Senegal, 8, 58–62, 159
Sennar, 9
Sere, 59
Settlers of Sierra Leone, 41
Seychelles Islands, 71
Sherbro Island, 51
Sibthorpe A. B. C., 44
Sierra Leone, 1, 6, 7, 40–50, 119,
135, 144–145
Sifawa, 17
Sinoe, 52
Slave trade, 5, 6
Sofa, 28
Sokoto, 9, 17, 37, 117
Songhai, 8
Soninke, 21
'Sons abroad' (of Sierra Leone), 44
Sori Biram, 25

Susu, 48

Tabin Kwaho, 15
Takoradi, 139
Takyiman, 64
Tantum, 71
Teda, 34
Tegbesu, King, 84
Tema, 156
Temne, 45
Thomson, Dr., 113
Tieba, 28
Tijaniyya, 22
Timbuktu, 9, 123
Togo, 36, 123, 158
Tokolor, empire, 21–31, 59
Trans-Saharan trade, 9
Trotter, Captain, 113
True Whigs (of Liberia), 54
Tuareg, 32

Uganda, 122
Umar, Al-Haji, 22–23
UNESCO, 151
United Gold Coast Convention
(U.G.C.C.), 142
Upper Guinea, 1, 3, 6
Upper Volta, 122, 129, 159
Urhobo, 91, 100
Usman dan Fodio, 9, 12–18, 37
Uzama, 92

Vai, 48

Wadai, 34
Walata, (Beeroo), 9
Warri, 7, 100
Wassa, 65
Watson Commission, 141
West African Examinations Council,
158
West African Frontier Force, 158
Western Sudan, 4, 8, 9, 12
Whydah, 8, 80, 110
Winneba, 71
Wolof, 59
Wolseley, Sir Garnet, 66, 70
World Bank, 151
World Health Organisation
(W.H.O.), 151